The Mythical Bird

"Rebirth of a Pious Daughter"

CHANDNI AKHENIA

First Published in August 2020

Published By:
Kalon Maple Publishing
+91 9665 609 444

ISBN:
9 788194 673965

Price: 199₹

Layout Design, Cover Design & Illustration:
Mrunaal Gawhande

Editor: Vivek Gawhande

Distributed by:
Paperback: amazon.com, amazon.in, flipkart, kalonmaplepublishing.com
E-Book: amazon.in/com, apple (ibooks stores in 51 countries), barnes & noble (us and uk), scribd, kobo, and blio, overdrive (world's largest library ebook platform serving 20,000 + libraries), baker & taylor axis 360, tolino, gardners, Google Play Books, bibliotheca cloud library (3,000 public libraries) and odilo (2,100public libraries in north america, south america and europe) +paperback

To the Phoenix in You.

Burn into Flames

And

Rise wiser with all the ashes.

ACKNOWLEDGEMENT

Before you begin to turn these pages, I would like to express my gratitude and cherish a few individuals who have been great influence and support in my life. Their presences have given me an opportunity to have a different outlook towards life. I'd like to appreciate my Parents, my sister Dhruvi Akhenia without whom this book could have been incomplete. A special thanks to Suyash Sharma who always inspired and had utmost confidence in me.

CONTENT

"Hope is the thing with feathers
that perches in the soul and sings the tune
without the words and never stops at all."

– Emily Dickinson

BEGINNINGS

Three years back I started with writing blogs just as college assignments. Isn't it like a turn of events that just from writing blogs I ended up writing a book. The blogs have always been about what we feel and tend to hide. Call it a mirror of facts. You can see a part of yourself in there while reading. Initially, I didn't realize that I had written about what a human feels. Gradually, I realized what we intend to hide. Still, I strongly believe in writing the actual truth.

So, I kept writing and will continue because as an individual it makes me feel right. Yes, I have written a lot for myself, maybe some advice, or maybe about the mistakes I made . Be it a fight with emotions or inner battles, Now, when I look back it feels like yes I have made it. I have changed for good. And with that I'm also proud about how I put up the things on the blog.

As an individual opening up to People has always been difficult for me. Log kya kahenge- fear of being misjudged, stereotypical norms, trust issues, self-doubt and social anxiety.. We tend to share our stories only with close friends and family. Each of us have our own story and they can be the same, related or different. All of us are imperfectly unique. Your past may hit you but it's a lesson learnt. Thereafter, there is no looking back. You got the eye of the tiger because, look how you have come all the way from zero to your own hero.

Alright, until I delve any further into the topic at hand, just like many of you, I'm just somebody who is passionate about writing and dreamed of being published one day.

Just like a coin our life has two sides. A positive and a negative. What we show is always the positive side and not the other side of the story.

Why do we do that? Because it's convenient. To show only the rosy aspects of life. And to be very honest we never ask the other side of the story too. So yes, let's talk about the other side of the story this time.

Life is a journey, a journey of a lot of experiences. Some experiences were good while some were bad. But problems are the part and parcel of life. They somehow make us stronger and wiser. Life is full of abrupt twists and turns. The moment you think everything is going smoothly and suddenly life takes a shift and all your plans and preparations are wasted. The little bubble we're living in bursts, and that's when we actually start living.

Indeed, these encounters are really unpleasant and often tragic. Yet everybody has bad experiences in life, and that's what makes them resilient enough to get through the challenges of life. Life isn't all about one moment; it's all about decades of experience. Through time and experience, the outlook continues to shift.

That's why it's better to just leave the past behind and look to the future with optimism and a little curiosity about what's waiting for you in the future. There will be slabs and thorns in your journey, and you will have to brush them aside to move forward.

With any unpleasant experience, we question why? It will only reinforce self-pity and not allow yourself to rise. You've got to take the pain with you and walk around with a million dollar smile and face it. There are many more chances that will come to you, and you will also have pleasant experiences.

So, don't you think we should make the most of the unpleasant experiences and be the individual to find the creative solution. Every life lesson we know, whether positive or negative, is a gem in personal growth.

EMPTINESS - A VOID

Emptiness isn't really emptiness. It still occupies a lot of space. A baggage of emptiness is heavy

Ever been in a situation wherein you have everything yet you feel that there is some part missing. A void, a gap that needs to be filled even when you have achieved whatever you wanted but still it feels like black hole as massive as a cliff. It feels like a desolate place within. In simple words, you feel hollow.

You're struggling to make sense of everything but you seem not to be able to do so because it's all rolled together in one huge plate. If you're trying to sort things out this pile will smash you underneath its power. You'll always drown in between such a chaos. Therefore, you keep things as they are in expectation that they will evolve miraculously. Yet rarely will they. So the pile, with all the stuff that you're trying to undo, just explodes like gas particles and you're left wondering where you've gone horribly wrong.

You encounter so numerous 'ifs' and 'maybe' and 'loopholes' that your head begins to spin and the pathway beyond tends to drift away, and you lose concentration. In a future that should have been as vibrant as the sun you see nothing but void. You see a saturation point on a journey you struggled so hard to walk. There are moments where you start confusing even more with the situations happening and then irrational decisions which make things even worse. You start drowning even more.

The feeling draws all the strength within you. It leaves you feeling like a worthless tank that has drained out. Void is the absence and dedication of emotional responses, it's not an emotion, it feels as if there is something missing in life, it just feels like it's all wrong, it feels confused on where life is going, it's the state you 're not willing to be in, and you likely won't set aside your brain.

Often, we experience a sense of loss inside. Looking inside, it seems there is nothing, so we surround ourselves with anything outside, like food or entertainment. And even these outward distractions only immediately take care of the emptiness; they only temporarily capture our focus. The Emptiness returns when the distraction is over. Emptiness is an emotional state that all individuals face periodically and it is not possible to walk away from it.

You feel the heaviness in your heart and the waves of chaos all in your head. If you feel empty, yet feel so heavy inside, toss away all that will impact you – your reason to worry, your anxieties, your expectations, everything which causes difficulty. Try and relax and just really vacate yourself from the heaviness of your heart.

Take it easy in your mind and focus only on what you're doing and what you want and need, instead of attempting to connect and sound right of all the scattered feelings. You have a remembrance of emotions but those emotions were overshadowed by silence. It's like somebody had a part omitted and then discarded it. You're still looking but you've no solution. You have moments of that.

There might be times when we feel empty for the longest time. But by working towards healing, bringing value and purpose to life, self-love leads to a happy life rather than being stuck in despair.

First of all, in order to really grasp this feeling of loss, you have to try to find the source. Explore deeply, and describe precisely what makes you feel this way it is? Is it because of the loss of a loved one? A heartbreak? Childhood traumatic event ? Or some painful memories. List and begin writing specific reasons that cause you to feel the hollowness. So, in a way you will spend some time connecting with your inner self.

You must name all the unpleasant feelings to relieve yourselves, and confront the suffering instead of trying to run away from it. Trying to push it away will only leave you feeling emptier, and will evolve in negative ways as time passes. It can be incredibly hard but as you continue to realize your emotions and let oneself feel them, you will ultimately find it a lot easier to deal with them. Take the time you need to heal yourself from the suffering by feeling it, and not criticizing yourself. Fill the void with compassion, love and care for yourself and others.

You may sense a void growing up since you haven't receive the love which you deserve, causing you to find it from someone else. That causes people to feel empty and disengaged from your soul when you lack self-love.

Fill in the gap by working unconditionally to love yourself, and not relying on someone else to fill the gap. When you start finding love in yourself, you wouldn't rely on it anymore.

To get rid of feeling empty, you need to start questioning what means you feel that way, and take the time to feel those experiences. You will start healing from it from there. Healing comes from oneself. You can't fill up the void with the other individuals or material products. But while recovery may still feel like it will get better with time! It takes some time to untangle and heal our emotional baggage and scars from the past.

But, there is a negative stigma to 'having a void,' there is also a positive side, as it can help you drill down into your inner consciousness, purpose and anything that could weigh you down. Though learning to cope with emotional pain may be challenging, when you do it will make you free from feeling empty and hook you up for much greater and worthwhile things you can encounter there.

Overthinking

Overthinking is like a Torture overpassing. It's hell to be stuck with a constant series of discomforting thoughts in your head. Over-thinking is like a slow poison. The brain is complicated; you have to think of not thinking about something in an attempt to think about something, to avoid thinking about it. It is desperate. We are overthinking since we are desperate creatures chasing answers. We like certitude and we like to be in charge. Don't worry its tactical aspect of human existence.

At any specific stage in life our thoughts can be driven in such a way that our view of the same set of circumstances changes from bright sunny to gloomy and thundery. And then, as we slip the sly slope of overthinking, our minds are overflowing with attacks like that. I've never thought about this," you probably might say this to yourself. So let me get this straight: You're constantly thinking, but you're never thinking of how much time your feelings sound like an addiction. I say that, because all of us are somewhere addicted to learning. Overthinking is a frequent problem but this can cause sleep disturbance, "thought anxiety," and even risk mental wellbeing when it gets out of hand. It is also a hard diagnosis, let alone cure.

The problem is many people don't recognize overthinking as an issue. If anyone criticizes overthinking, we sometimes conclude that through pessimistic thoughts the issue dwells on or spirals. At the same token, we prefer to think optimistic thoughts are healthy. Yet to presume that all the optimistic thoughts are healthy is a mistake.

What most recommendations on self-help says is to kill the negative emotions and double on the positive thoughts. This, on the surface, sounds like a good advice. Yet the fact is that it can get blocked up much like a drain when you overdo your brain, for either positive or negative end result. That results in bad decision-making.

You 're not your thoughts; thinking is not considered a habit of curbing, since it is so closely related to our core identities. In Meditation, nobody said it better than Marcus Aurelius: "Our life is what our thoughts make it." What he is saying is that the nature of our thoughts shapes our lives. I believe it. Many of us, though, believe we are our reflections.

We usually say: "Well I can't help but think about things. You can decide what thoughts you wish to forget. "It's just me". "No, you are not". I like how Eckhart Tolle puts it in The Power of Now: "The beginning of freedom is the realization that you are not the possessing entity — the thinker."

The best way to prevent engaging with your feelings is to avoid all the feelings being carried through. Alternatively, try to live in the present moment — where you have little time to ponder, only to feel. Instead of actively using the tool for 16 or 17 hours while you're wide awake, take it to use when you need it. Instead of overthinking why don't we strike that same energy towards our goals? That same amount of energy in understanding what is causing you to think about that one thought. Start observing the thoughts you have.

Restrict your thoughts to periods of commitment. For instance, sit down and really focus while journalizing or setting your everyday goals. Give yourself some clear time — say, 15 to 30 minutes. It is perfectly fine to follow through with your feelings during those moments. What we try to avoid is excessive thoughts. Let go of all your worries about the past and future. No matter how much you want to do in the future, and no matter how much you have suffered in the past, appreciate being safe and healthy right now.

"It's okay to be bothered by the negativity that affects us, we're all human, but it's important to realize that we need to let go of it in the end! REMEMBER TO PUT DOWN THE Bottle! Because the longer you hold the bottle it will only keep getting heavier. The question that we need to ask ourselves is- Why do I choose to suffer when I can let it go?

Don't think of your failures or things or what's going to happen tomorrow. I'm here, just now. Just like the moment you take in reading these words. It's forever gone when that's done. Realize that, in a subconscious way you will never dare to flee the present.

Overthinking is not less than a torture. A place where all the discomforting thoughts keep running through your mind. A phase where all your negative thoughts take over the positive thoughts. And it starts taking the control.

Self-Doubt
- The Enemy of Your Abilities

"What if I fail?"
"Oh... But darling..! What if you fly?"

Have you ever questioned your decisions or your capability? Do you still think about things you want to do yourself? Would you like to feel more comfortable about going after your goals and building your ultimate life? Okay, but then you decide to enhance your professional life, personal relationships or physical wellbeing, something will hold you back. You can't start taking steps because you have questions about yourself. You're too afraid to step forward because within, you think you're already a failure, or you're too concerned about the repercussions that could happen.

I strongly believe that we all have that little inner voice that tells us what we want to do with our lives and who we want to be. Sadly, we're putting this inner voice aside and we're beginning to think stuff like, "How am I going to make the money out of this? "What are people going to think of me? "And" What happens if I fail? "

We often hold back from achieving things that we believe will bring real meaning and intent to our lives, since there is this underlying fear that we are not good enough. Whether it's about our skills, our capability, our public persona, or the way we do things on a regular basis, self-doubt is always nagging us in the back of our minds.

Often, we find ourselves in a situation where we have a clear vision about what we want from our life and feel ready to move forward, but self-doubt can be the fastest way to slow you down. If you believe the inner voice of doubt, it can easily rob you of your motivation, create fear, and contradict all the planning you have made to achieve your goal. So, at some stage along your path, it becomes necessary to shift self-doubt into faith.

Little did we know that self-doubt and fear go hand in hand, and together they undermine trust. When we fear that we'll be punished for our failures, self-doubt comes to stop us from taking chances so we won't get to that point.

We subconsciously understand the sequence of self-doubt as some kind of protection from failure. Together, fear and self-doubt keep us invulnerable and unsatisfied, and that is the opposite of what we are.

There is self-doubt whenever we want to make changes in life. It could be a better job, a different life scenario, a better diet, or a romantic relationship. There's this feeling within you and that there's more to life than you're actually living now.

Yet for some reason, we doubt that we deserve to have the life that you're dreaming of. We doubt that we are going to have the motivation, dedication, emotional maturity, or persistence to make things work. You think of everything that could be wrong instead of what could be right.

Everyone's got a story. Story of how the past molded us to be who we are presently. And we have tales that we make up in our minds, excessively.

These stories are from things that have happened in the past. They come from events where some other people have criticized us for. They come from presumptions of us and the future, too. We start to believe that these facts are real no matter what.

For instance, you might have given a presentation in college and it failed poorly. Maybe someone from the group told you that you were awful when you gave the presentation. Because of one instance, you feel like you're never going to be good at giving presentations for the rest of your life. There are times when you feel you aren't smart enough, pretty enough or maybe not good for a relationship. All of this just because of that one event in our life. We let that one event be so impactful that we start doubting ourselves and keep questioning ourselves.

Self-doubt can be a disturbing and persuasive voice that holds you back. It stops you from taking advantage of your opportunities. It makes it harder to get going or finish activities that we need to. I won't be denying the fact that there are times when I have been questioning myself.

Do what makes you happy rather than taking a step back. Do it. Even if it's not 100% great or amazing.

What's essential is to keep doing what you love to do and remember this quote: "Doubt kills more dreams than even failure can't. keep on dreaming. Keep doing this. Especially on the days when you start to realize the lies that say you're not good enough for this world. It's a horrendous, heartbreaking lie, and the world really needs your glow in it.

We've got the ability to rewrite our own story. You're going to know who you want to be and what you're going to do with your career, relationships, professional life and so on. This comes down to three things: believing yourself, changing your attitude, and taking baby steps.

The first step to start dealing with self-doubt is to start believing yourself and not the opinions which people have for us. Overcoming self-doubt is all about building trust and confidence. You need to trust your gut, your journey, and your feelings. Trust that you're going to get where you want to be. If you know that it is what you need to do inside of your heart and intuition, you need to follow that.

Ever since you start realizing that you have all the power inside of you, you can take responsibility for the consequences and decisions and do the powerful stuff anyway. It all gets down to your thought process or whether you believe that you are capable of receiving the things you want to see in your life.

I know there's many reasons that make you trust yourself, but honestly, it's all about you. Work on your mind, give more attention to your mental well-being, and look for ways to be a lot, a lot more generous on oneself. Rephrase every story which tells you that if you're not good enough.

Without sounding cheesy I would tell you this, you're good enough. If you're not doing things that worry you merely because of fear, it's not a good excuse.

I wouldn't want to see you lounging around, feeling trapped and unhappy because you're afraid to make that big jump into something that might really make you smile. I would like you to start taking such tiny steps and make things work someday, instead of not before.

"Look within; You are more than what you have become"
Like a cyclone the questions were running in her mind;
Am I good enough?
Am I beautiful?
Am I unkind?

She closed her eyes forming an ocean door
And realized it was all just in her head and she let those waves go to the shore; she was perfect with all her imperfections and that's how she bid byes, to the cyclone of Self-Doubt inside her mind."

Self-Doubt cages you. Set yourself free from the cage of self-doubt and let yourself bloom like flowers

Emotions
- A Game of Snakes
and ladders.

Tum agar khulke ro nahi sakogi ...
Toh khulkar has kaise sakogi?

Haven't we all heard this popular dialogue? For people, feelings and emotions are very much the same. So naturally, we would perceive them as synonyms; two words with the same meaning. However, they are dependent on each other, emotions and feelings are different things.

Emotions describe psychological state and are generated subconsciously. Usually, they are bodily responses to certain events. By contrast, feelings are basically subjective experiences of emotions driven by conscious thoughts and reflections. It states we can have emotions without having feelings, however, one simply cannot have feelings without having emotions.

Emotions... How should I describe them? A roller- coaster ride? Or maybe an explosion of chemicals in our body mentally or the way I explained it above. Though we know our mind and heart are located at different places but they are intimately connected, Too much science Huh! (Difficult). Let's keep it simple because we complicate things. So, a roller coaster sounds perfect.

Emotions can construct and at the same time cause destruction. Emotions keep us from seeing a broader picture of the world. And at the same time, feelings are a wider context, or at least a major part of a big picture. And then it begins.. Starting from childhood we start understanding the emotions of happiness, sadness. Aren't they the most talked about? No one talks about the other emotions, jealousy, envy, insecurities, fear, guilt and the list goes on. We are still confused about the difference between jealousy and envy. But we know every broken thing can be mended and it's never too late.

In a way, emotions are what makes us one of the most individual. Emotions, five simple yet so complicated emotions or like I said we complicate things. A messenger of feelings in your heart and mind. Let's not dive into the complexity of emotions. Little did we know how logic and emotions go and in hand.

We can't really think without emotion, thinking logically doesn't suggest thinking without emotion. Emotions have logic on their own.

In The Humans, Matt Haig said, "Without emotions humans would not care for each other, and if they did not care for each other, the species would have died out. Caring for others is self-preservation. You take care of someone and they take care of you. "Emotions are not meant to be understood as logic, they are meant to be recognized and considered.

All of us have different patterns of emotions but they are unpredictable. For instance, if you are happy you express it in different forms likewise happens when you're upset. Maybe you would just have a cup of coffee or maybe a good walk or nap (everyone's favorite). Do you know what evokes the human emotions the most? Music. evoque range of human emotions right from being sad, nostalgic, and tense, to happy, calm, and joyous. (Just saying) and everyone would have a different emotion for the song.

As we know, emotions can construct us and destroy us. Being too emotional and being irrational about emotions can cause imbalance and understanding your emotions might even take a whole lifetime. But you know what? Life is too short to understand the complexity of emotions so rather than understanding them why can't we feel them with all the freedom.

But, life comes with ifs and buts. We humans tend not to express our emotions. Do we express? No we don't. We never do. Why? I myself don't have an answer to this, but all I know is we suppress them. Don't we ? Suppressing emotions is like a feeling where you're in a jar with storms and, and a lot of chaos, restlessness, anxiety and what not. And the best way to be at peace is never deny your emotions, never deny what you feel, be it positive or negative. NEVER DO THAT.

When we hold on to the unsaid emotions it doesn't let us function gracefully. Why? Because we carry the baggage of fears, sadness. It is a difficult process.

Be it learning and unlearning but that's what keeps us moving right? And we aren't robots who won't feel. We are humans and yes we can express. We just need to open up about what we feel.

Showing your emotions doesn't make you weak, be it men or women. We must agree wholeheartedly with all of that. All sexes, particularly men, should be able to show their feelings without being shamed and judged for it. We are human so we are embedded with emotional responses as human beings and therefore we shouldn't keep them in because it only creates more problems later. People do believe that expressing your feelings is vulnerability, especially if you are a man however that's not the case.

It is a big sign of strength and courage because you are willing to show but not run from such feelings. Showing emotions is just a part of being human and therefore we shouldn't judge other people for expressing how they feel, even though that's what we do as humans in the longer term. We come from a culture that is clinging on to taboos and the way these things were for other spans of time. Men are always told that it would be a weakness to show your emotions and say what you feel without any hesitation but that's not the way it should be.

That's why men hide their feelings because of stigmas associated with them. Men are being taught to be tough enough to carry their own emotional states, but overtime it has shifted, although many people actually believe it is a weak point to show your feelings and thoughts. And there is nothing more important than sharing how you feel, and allowing others to know what your emotions are.

That is a tremendous symbol of courage and strength. It is something that needs to improve because their feelings should not be covered regardless of how others view them. Within this world we all need to work together to support one another and we don't need to demolish people to take the step to show courage to share their emotions.

Emotions are our own to be invested in. If we don't find ways to find them before they show up unsung, they're going to cause destruction. When we open our hearts and minds to a bigger picture, a meaningful life, we are ready to create who we really are and the life we really want.

We just don't want to lose ourselves until we find ourselves. We're just what we hear. We do, however, share one unspeakable, universal feeling; wonder that is a wider picture.

Emotions- A war within.

Emotions are like the game of snakes and ladders. Difficult to identify. A maze of confusion.

Insecurities
- The Root Cause Of All

I read it somewhere
- "Unfollow everything that makes you feel like you need to be someone else"

"Confidence is silent while Insecurities are loud."

It says it all. We never talk about them while some are open about them (not many maybe one or two) while the rest 99% never accept the insecurities they have. You will be surprised by the number of people around you who are suffering from insecurities. It might be you with the insecurities. Or the girl who seems to have everything right in life. The insecurity is all around us. But most people won't even care if you've put up a huge sign and tossed it around.

Well, deep down we also know what it is like to feel as insecure as an email password. The feeling where even if you know the answer you don't answer it (fear) what if the answer is wrong, what if they laugh?

Name it social anxiety, self-confidence, or inhibition. Whatever we name it; insecurities are a fundamental part of the human condition. Often you wonder if anyone likes you, If you're just going to be content with yourself. If you can't be happy with yourself, would anyone be happy with you? It's going to make you nervous. It's a constant loop of fear, low self-esteem, and anxiety. A loop that slowly and unknowingly kills who you are.

You might be thinking if I have insecurities or not. Yes, I do have insecurities and I have spent half of my life being insecure (I still do feel at times). Insecurities in general start with the way you look, the way you dress, about your body as well, the skin, the skin color. It all starts with the comparison either you yourself does it or people are always there to make us feel so. It makes you feel like shit, not good enough for things or someone. It's the worst feeling I know.

Insecurity makes it hard for us to voice our opinions, to make us incapable of dissenting, and to make us uncertain in our professional relationships. It leaves us unsatisfied, weakens cooperation and tends to make our teams less creative and efficient. If there is an enemy of authenticity and creativity, it is fear. No wonder we're trying so hard to get rid of it.

Insecurity can be a resource which will always bring you to your knees in the fight against your foe. Why? Why? Since your defense is the heel of your Achilles (You can google this). Insecurities as I said we don't talk about it. So what we do is we keep bottling things within and it suffocates you and kills you little by little and if we ever think about sharing, there is another thought running in the back of our mind. So it goes in two ways.

Number one- While some of us decide to tell it to someone. They'd probably laugh about your insecurities (or otherwise) and make you feel guiltier. Unfortunately, it makes you feel even more terrible.

Number two- Bottle it up and make things worse again. You'd sense the rising fear inside of you. And No one would have helped since they didn't know about it.

Insecurities are caused by three reasons: It can be the events caused in childhood which later starts showing its impact during the teenage years. For instance: In childhood someone abandoned you while you were knocking the door crying and screaming to let you in. During childhood it has a very strong impact on your mind but with time we tend to forget that memory is suppressed. And when you grow up you feel like not being good enough or missing out. In other words you feel FOMO "The Fear of Missing Out'. The other reason could be, when your trust is broken. Last but not the least, comparing you with someone. They are three major factors which cause insecurities. Little did we know, that there are a number of insecurities we have and we deal with them.

So, let's dive into the most types of insecurities. Insecurities are full of IF's and BUT's. Not only girls but even boys do face insecurities when it comes to their bodies.

Don't you think that you are too fat for this dress? God you're so skinny just like a matchstick. You have so many curves. You don't have curves. You have too many flabs and you need to reduce your weight. All of us might have gotten such comments many times.

Why do we criticize someone's body so much? Are you perfect? Obviously NOT. Actually no one is. We all have flaws. Do we still need to be taught that BODY SHAMING IS NOT RIGHT?

Being fat won't make you ugly nor would being skinny make you feel that. But yes, the comments make people feel so. The comments make one feel ugly or hate themselves. Being fat, skinny or curvy is not a crime. It's just how their body is, If they are comfortable in their skin why do we need to give them opinions you need to reduce or you need to eat more. When you call someone fat or skinny you make them uncomfortable in their own skin.

Just because you have a thigh gap or a toned stomach doesn't mean you are pretty on the inside, what matters is your soul. Never underestimate yourself by saying, I wish I had a body like hers" or by calling yourself "Ugly".

Remember one thing everyone is BEAUTIFUL. Embrace your bodies and love them because body confidence doesn't come from trying to achieve a great body, but by embracing the one you already have.

SEXUAL INSECURITIES

When it comes to romantic relationships, there are several peculiar complexities that individuals struggle with. Yet they never express it to their partner about it.

Young or old, gay or homosexual, there's nothing like making you think your mate is on the verge towards granting your relationship a little push. Will he be betraying you? Is he flirting around? Did you think your partner is cheating on you? Are you suspecting him or her of such things? We may have reasons to be worried, so here's another explanation: most of us, for a number of reasons, consciously or unconsciously or deliberately build feelings of insecurity in our relationships as a way to regain the love that we once had.

Insecurity can be strong. You're unrestrained in love, showing him your finest bits so his interest doesn't wander around. He's going to see you all in terms of proving without a doubt it's you he likes. But, while suspicion and speculation can inject heat into a normal relationship, they can also create unnecessary tension, which is worn down by both you and your partner.

Let's take a quick look at the path of insecurity in a relationship of commitment. First of all, this uncertainty will show itself outside the bedroom as intense envy, and manifest itself as increased sensitivity and criticism of how the partner deals with others.

Sex and anxiety go hand in hand more like shoes and flip flops. Well, agree or not, every one of us is insecure somewhere. Sexual insecurity has a major impact on our sex lives, relationships and self-esteem. Anxiety can cause a number of symptoms of sexual problems. How is that? It is when anxiety hijacks your brain and nervous system, producing a surge of chemicals and stimulation that throws you into battle-or-flight mode. It's impossible to have sex in this state because, on a biological level, your central nervous system is pushing your body to defeat or run away – not to commit fornication.

Body Image Issues are becoming an increasingly common cause of sexual anxiety among men. Why wouldn't I want to be bigger, slimmer and more ripped? Studies have found that most of us are uncomfortable with our bodies, and a quarter of people tend to also have light sex as a result. Apart from having a negative effect on your personal life, these kind of problems are linked to self-esteem issues, food disorders , depression and more. However, no one should be ashamed of their bodies, so if that gives you serious anxiety or hinders your ability to lead a regular life but adapting a healthier lifestyle in terms of diet, exercise and sleep habits will help you transform the way you feel about yourself by growing self-esteem and motivation.

Satisfying Your Partner Sexually. Why are we so hung up on this? Especially, when it's not actually a bad thing. Men desperately want their partners to orgasm because that helps them feel more manly. We're obsessed with offering orgasms since we care for our partners, and also because we're tangled up in our own fragility. Note that, entering sex with an orgasm at the end is not the end of everything. Instead, we need to concentrate on developing an atmosphere of shared enjoyment. Sexually, this also involves spending more on foreplay. But don't limit yourself to that: a satisfying sex life is founded on deep emotional foundations. Look for happiness by giving her a massage, preparing her a meal, and giving your undivided attention to her day. All of this will relieve the strain and make you understand that your relationship will be incredibly rewarding, even though it doesn't intensify every time.

Not only this, but men also face the performance related anxiety and the biggest concern is that a mere case of erectile dysfunction is often enough to make a man nervous whether or not he will get an erection every time he wants to have sex. Following a poor sexual experience or two, you could find yourself back in your sexual performance anxiety loop, which is a task to get over.

It's okay to think about being able to get it or keep it up. But with the concern of how fear affects your brain, worrying about your erection limits your ability to get one.

Whether or not you have already been diagnosed with erectile dysfunction, the easiest way to overcome this specific source of vulnerability is by addressing the underlying sexual performance anxiety that triggers erectile problems.

Talking about women and her sexual insecurities. Well, when a girl tells you she's never had a sexually insecure moment in her whole life, she's lying. It's like claiming you've never been hungry. We were all thirsty, exhausted, and furious. So, we were both physically unhealthy.

Women usually are worried about being perfectly groomed, the way they smell.

Many men don't really know that you have perfectly flat, hairless legs as you get hot and sweaty under the covers. They become much more interested in the heat of the moment. You're a hell of a lot better than just a few hairs in your gorgeous entirety. Most of us had this vulnerability. Mainly because culture has pounded into us that our perfect female looks like Hell.

Oh, girl. That is not so as long as you are a healthy person with daily bathing habits, you are perfect.

Insecurity is part and parcel of life, be it for men or women, though very few of us can talk about it. It's important that we get comfortable with those parts of ourselves that don't measure up to what our culture feels is masculine and feminine. One way to achieve so is by reflecting on an issue that so many people are painfully conscious of: sexual vulnerability. When we are able to embrace sexual insecurities that we have addressed , we will be able to develop our own sex lives while also strengthening our relationships and ultimately being better people by becoming more open, truthful and self-aware.

PROFESSIONAL AND ECONOMIC INSECURITIES

Don't you think that they go hand in hand? If you don't have a job you'll feel financially insecure and that will make you think about what if I lose my job? And that's the pint when we develop Professional and Economic "Financial" Insecurities. However, financial insecurities can be caused even due to bad investments.

Professional insecurity consists of the fear of losing your job, being denied tenure or any restrictions that you may face at your place of work for failing to comply with the established guidelines. This vulnerability is exacerbated by the great demands of life in terms of finance. Losing a job means losing income, making it one of the most common forms of insecurity.

Also recognized as financial insecurity, economic uncertainty revolves around your financial capability or inability to do so. It's the fear that you might be wasting your money instead of saving it. This also includes the fear of making a poor investment. Also, you are socially or financially insecure because you feel that you will not have enough money to sustain your standard of living.

INSECURITIES IN RELATIONSHIPS

Are you are constantly concerned about whether your partner really loves you? Are they cheating or betraying you in some other way? Relationship uncertainty can be damaging and a simple way to destroy future happiness. These emotions can lead to an extremely unhealthy relationship situation. Not just the person who feels uncertain, not experiencing happiness, but the person's partner is likely to suffer as well. Insecurity in a relationship is not always a feature of the relationship itself. The root of these feelings also comes from something encountered in the past. Such past experiences build a conceptual structure for how we interpret both present and future experiences. There are certain events in life which leave deep and strong imprints on us emotionally and mentally.

People are not only insecure about their weight, don't let me contradict you; weight is a massive struggle for a lot of people, that's why I spent a whole paragraph thinking about it. Many people are confused about the hair color or texture, freckles or lack of hair, lack of excess muscle, etc. Such uncertainties are absolutely natural, and I assure you, they're a lot more common than you think they are. What you've got to know is that you're never ever going to see yourself the way other people see you. It has been proved that we tend to see ourselves in a far worse way than we see others; for instance A girl with freckles wishes for a clear skin while the girl with clear skin wishes for freckles " That girl is me by the way".

We've been wasting so much time worrying about what we don't have and forget to appreciate what we have. We have people who think we're beautiful, even on our worst days.

"The reason we struggle with insecurity is because we compare our behind the scenes with everyone else's highlight reel."

- Steve Furtick

This urge to be liked has grown even more in today's social media age. The number of followers and likes that a person has on their Instagram account determines how popular they are. Particularly, if those followers and likes are rigid and paid for. Competition is growing up, and all we're fighting for are numbers that define our place in life. Social media is a part of our everyday lives. The medium is intended to be fun and exciting. Documenting and sharing your life with an audience is the most incredible thing you've ever done. It's almost like a diary of every day. The fear of missing out (FOMO) is another phobia that exists in today's social media youth. This happens when an individual sees another individual's lavish lifestyle on social media but little did we know that these smiling face on social media are not always true.

Girls feel far more uncertain about their social media activity. They're always making sure they look slim and comfortable in a photo, that their make-up is on the mark, and they're not revealing too much skin. Comments are typically harsh and judgmental on a girl's profile page. This has negative effects on both their physical and mental health.

If they're going to be spotted by someone in real life, they need to convince people that they are just the same as they are on social media. The most popular concern is that she's called out, "She doesn't look like her Instagram images." We are actively seeking the approval of others to affirm ourselves. We're worrying, if we don't get more than 50 likes on a photo we shared an hour ago, some people have recourse to taking their picture down.

We're going out of the way to make our lives seem even more appealing to our followers. Not understanding that we are making ourselves an individual for people to like us, and not disclosing the real. Social media profiles reflect a person's personality and how they are in real life.

Spread positive remarks about people's social media feeds. Put on the uniqueness of social media. At the end of the day, you're in control of your happiness; don't let those harsh comments come to you.

I know that thinking about insecurities and how normal they are won't erase them from your mind; that's just not how this whole "human being" thing works. But you should remember even in your toughest days, you are beautiful and adored; even when you feel the rain falling on your back, the sun is coming that will warm you up again.

And even if you may not feel good enough right now, it doesn't mean you're not. If you are around people who make you feel bad, get away from them and start hanging out with positive people who pick you up while you're down.

Maybe in today's world looking happy has turned out to be more important than actually being happy.

Read this somewhere

One should start following artists rather than following influencers! Why? Your entire outlook on life will change. It will remind you less about your insecurities. Instead you'll be reminded more what you love about humans and what humans are capable of creating.

Suggestion- *Why keep it bottled up? Maintain a journal and it will be your listener. Where you could pour in every thought you have, your feelings, about how your day was, good and bad things. Because your journal won't be judging you like how people do. Also it won't complain and won't demand. Trust me writing about your feelings will make you feel better. It won't make a joke out of your insecurities or use it as a weapon against you to put you down. Your journal will always be there by you.*

Embrace yourself with all the imperfections

FOMO
- Replace it with inner peace.

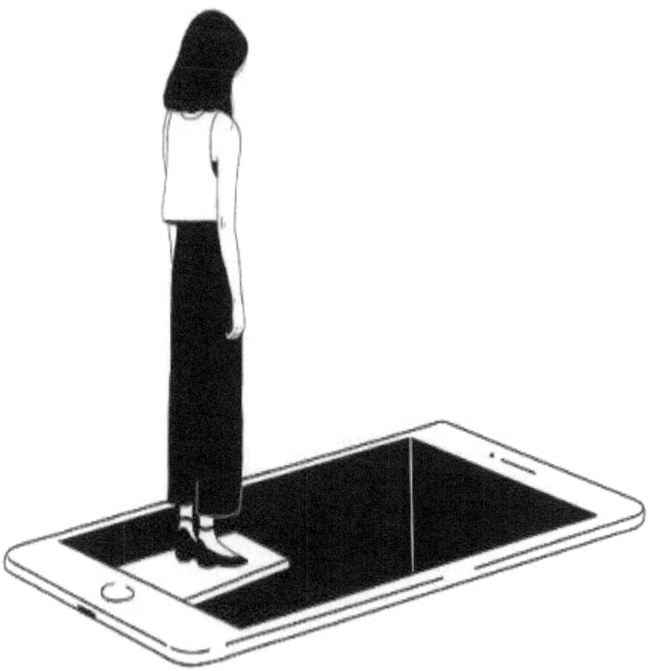

"Not everything on social media is the truth"

Talking about fears. You might, of course, think about varied incarnations of fear, such as fear of bugs, or maybe some other insect, or our incredible capacity to visualize and fear at any point in time. Or at all, the fear of airplanes. But no, no! FOMO is one of the most known phobias of these days. As a fear of missing something, that's a fear of missing something.

FOMO, The fear of missing out is one of the most increasing phobias in this digital era. It causes a different sort of stress into us, an anxiety which keeps on eating you from within. Let's make it a little more simple to understand this FOMO is basically feeling alone together.

Fear of missing out relates to the feeling or belief that others are having more fun, living better lives, or doing more than you are. It involves a deep sense of jealousy, and it affects self-esteem. Social networking platforms like Instagram and Twitter are also exacerbated.

FOMO is the anxiety that makes us believe that others might have pleasant feelings that we're missing out on. That has an effect on several of the choices we make in our everyday lives, even those involving money. It has existed for a long time, but we sense this more today thanks to agents like social networking sites. It can be troublesome if it starts to influence your daily routine and lifestyles and behavior.

How many times are you checking your phone every day? How many of us need to check out social media? In reality, has it caused you agony to keep up with the (good) life of other people? FOMO ("Fear of Losing Out," fear of missing something, in Portuguese) is an emotion generated by thinking that gives rise to anxiety and even depression. The restless feeling that you're missing something that others are doing, and certainly you are missing it on.

FOMO impacts people of all ages in different ways. However, for uber-digital youth, FOMO can be particularly hard hit. Seeing a friend's Paris holiday photos on Instagram or seeing friends at a Snapchat party can give rise to emotions of disappointment and isolation that can cause anxiety and even depression. FOMO typically happens when we feel we aren't involved in an activity.

Creating the fear of missing something in the online world, a person feels the need to constantly update social media to keep themselves aware of what others are doing. For example, check out Facebook every five minutes, go to an event that thinks about Instagram posts, or roll the Twitter timeline even if they don't have more news.

Just as you can have access to what other lives have, we could struggle because we don't have the life that we wanted. This social agony is primarily triggered by the fact that the user 's interaction with technology is still very fresh and inexperienced.

The problem arises when you envy what another does and that will paralyze you. The more we concentrate on others, what he/she has, and what we don't have, the less we get and we are left with the less imaginative feeling about our life. We prevent ourselves from creating anything that's good for self. We need to concentrate on finding happiness with what is ours and what we are creating.

FOMO, Fear Of Missing Out, is a growing epidemic in which people overpower and fail to meet their promises and choose to deflect blame as much as possible. We are wired to make a social bond and need to be part of it. However, this fear of missing out on the social bond has led to perfectionism and the need to control our social ties. We're almost obsessed with doing everything and being connected at all times. The truth is that we can't be everywhere all the time.

Why can't we Redefine your perceptions about our self and accept that we don't need to do it all and practice gratitude while you're in the moment. Somewhere, we end up losing our own identity while creating an entire different identity for the online world or in simplistic words or in simple words to match the people living a perfect life on social media.

Remember, the grass on the other side is not always greener. Whatever you've got right now, what you've been doing right now, and who you're with right now, is exactly where you meant to be.

FOMO! Fear of Missing Out. One of the most heard word these. A virtual world tieing us up with unrealistic expectations. Be it looks, lifestyle, body and lot more. A world where we are tied up around all the social media apps and internet.

Guilt
-The Slow Poison

"Guilt the thief of life"

Guilt is a feeling that people usually have after doing something wrong, deliberately or inadvertently. A person's sense of guilt typically refers to one's belief system. Guilt isn't necessarily bad. It's also positive sometimes. Feeling bad after making the wrong decision can lead to an improvement, such as an apology or a decision to make a better choice in the future.

It's not always easy to understand what guilt is. In reality, guilt and shame are often confused with one another, even though they are different emotions. Guilt defines a sense of regret or responsibility that refers to the action taken. While "Guilt says I did wrong. Shame says I am wrong."

Once in a lifetime, we all find ourselves in scenarios where someone has done something that affects us, and it's important to be able to discern whether or not their apology is valid or not. Here I am not being nit-picky when I say we just need to actively look for. In order to understand that the answer of the wrongdoer is real and meaningful, we must observe carefully. We need to listen closely to what the person says and what he or she does subsequently.

Guilt is an extremely powerful emotion. There's a wide range of stuff to feel bad about — from feeling guilty about someone you've hurt in your childhood, For not making the most of your time when it was time, and much more. Many may wonder how our mental health is influenced by guilt. Will it affect us in the long run, and how bad can it be? Let's take a closer look at this.

The sense of guilt is unique from feeling sad or upset – guilt often combines feelings of shame, anxiety, frustration, and humiliation. These emotions can go well inside and build up over time, especially if we never admit to ourselves that we were at fault. Guilt can have a major impact on our feeling of self-worth and self-esteem. Guilt is not a pleasant feeling to get through, but has a purpose. It keeps you away from entering a cycle of actions that are not good for you and others.

If this action happens, the shame in you works like a brake so that you don't continue to do the same thing. Guilt is only for the right amount and just for that period of time. If it goes past a limit, it eats you up like the termites are chewing you completely.

Guilt's that relate to past mistakes or failures can set an individual up for continued struggle. Often guilt may also prevent a person from having a good relationship with others.

Guilt, when rightly observed, can help to guide a person's values and help people grow and learn from mistakes. For example, if you cheat on a test and feel bad, you may discover that this is not the way you want to be and decide to make different choices in the future. When you say anything that hurt someone's feelings, you can go on to apologize and deepen your relationship.

Guilt is like that one mistake which feels like something that keeps pinching you. It's the pinch that irks the consciousness, and the pinch disallows the mistake to be repeated. Be with the pain, not the shame. It will also stop you from doing it again. Your very desire to repent has resolved the target. This wish is a warning that your intellect is ripening. Otherwise, you wouldn't have been aware of your behavior.

Actually, in the Covid- 19 when all are locked up in our homes. Where we have this whole time to do things we always wanted to do, we might have also thought of hurt or damage we have done to someone previously. Like you're in a really happy zone, and then this one thought randomly from the past, and here we go. The guilt trip begins. We might have felt this at least once.

We usually feel guilty when we hurt others. Maybe we don't realize it at that particular time. But in the later stage we do realize the damage we have caused to someone. But do you know which is the worst damage? The damage done to yourself. It happens when you prioritize everyone before yourself. Everyone's happiness before your happiness. You give so much to people that there comes a time where you feel empty. All you can feel is the guilt. In simple words you betray yourself.

Lastly in Mahabharata, Krishna says to Arjun, "I will alleviate you of your sins. You just surrender to me. Then it is my responsibility to take care of your sins. Don't worry about anything. Break all you're holding on to — even your dharma. "What you have to do is let go of all you're holding on to".

Guilt- A demon strangling within you
Feeling like a knot in my throat a gunpowder already rolled which is about to explode

Self-Betrayal
- The Breaking of the Chain

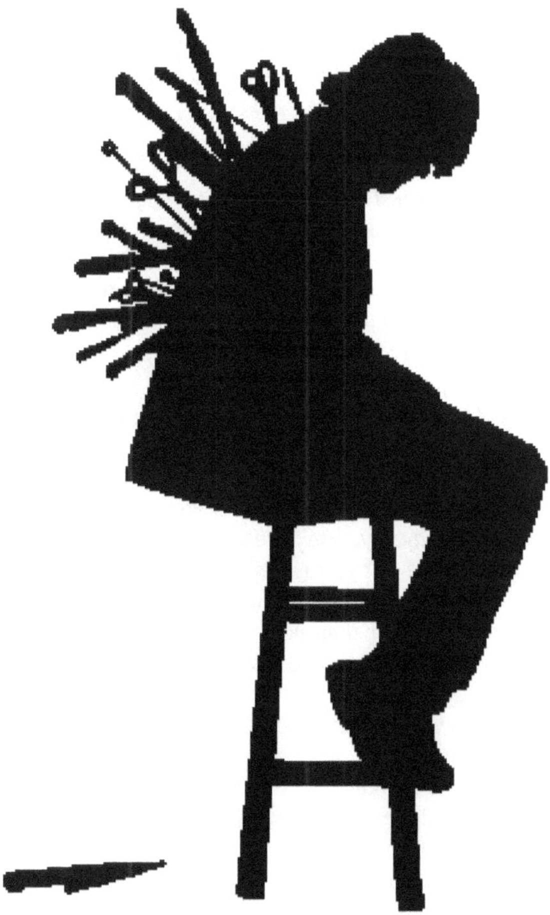

Let's proceed with a question. If someone questions you who are the four most significant people in life? You're quick to tell people who are important to you. But look on the other side. You 'll forget yourself. We often cross oceans and oceans for people in our lives. But, do they do the same for you?

For instance, what If every person was born with a seed planted deeply in their heart, how often would people tend to that seed, nourish it, and let it flourish? And if the seed had begun to grow into a pine tree, but the person saw that everyone else was beginning to develop pine trees? Would they try hiding the palm tree to blend in? Would they go so far as to kill it?

Self-betrayal is just a type of suicide. People often fear rejection by society, the norms, or just by the feeling of being lonely and not being accepted by the people around. We give priority to other people so much that we tend to neglect about our wellbeing. We've been conditioned since childhood in a way we're supposed to see what makes someone else smile. Perhaps, we also think that we've spent half of our lives living for the people around us. For instance, the one kid your parents want "The Honhaar Baccha" , the perfect girlfriend or the best husband. Talking about betrayal from people ? Well, in that case that harsh truth is that no one betrays us as much as we betray our own selves.

You've had a number of situations that you mark as betrayal. And in those times, you betrayed yourself even before another person made the choices that you made felt betrayed. You deceived self by saying " yes "when you wanted to say" no; "not standing openly; caring more for the happiness of others rather than your own; and just not having a voice when you are a voice. Self-betrayal has become an epidemic.

When we grow up, we are led to believe that we need to be different in order to receive love. So, when we are not our true self, we betray ourselves. Every time we hold back our emotions because we've been told that we're too fragile, each time we filter ourselves since we're "too young," but every time we make choices based on "what our parents wanted" we ignore who we really are and deceive ourselves.

We forget about ourselves in the process of making everyone else happy. How we'd like to do with a life or a future one would like to lead. You might have heard this statement, "Main sab ko samajhta hu par mujhe koi bhi nahi," that might sound right to the point, but the reality is that nobody is going to understand you. First, you need to comprehend yourself. Prioritize yourself over everyone. Do what fills your heart with joy. Laugh till your stomach hurts. A life you would want. Self-betrayal is generally the fruit of the undergrown tree. We have learned that our well-being is inaccurate, and that it is spatially lower than the well-being of everyone else. The cluster of wounds looks like being totally reliant on others, impeachment of own needs, unhappy or disorganized attachment, external control locus, focus on the other person, rationalizing.

Many of us take a glance out for answers — never having learned to believe what's inside. Even though we've never experienced, it can be hard to say what we feel, what we like and also what we don't like.

*As we work to heal this, it can be especially hard to trust oneself, particularly if we have an unpopular view. We might say, "Ok, I * should * be wrong because everybody else feels different!" It's going to be harder when people that disagree with you and are people you adore, trust, respect, or deeply respect. It is ever more enticing to forsake our own wisdom, opinions, and preferences.*

Self-betrayal expresses "DENIAL OF OUR OWN REALITY": we see something happening and still deny or avoid situations. In simple words, we discover that we cannot accept our own perceptions + that rejection of circumstances / breakdown in communication is how we cope with problems. Ignoring Our OWN Desires: our core human wants and needs are to be seen, heard, and genuinely expressed. We have physical, emotional , and spiritual needs. If our guardians will not teach by modeling that we can have a need + another human being requires the needs to be fulfilled, we can compromise our own desires. Many of us don't know what our desires are.

We teach ourselves how to treat ourselves in the manner we treat ourselves. How do we demand others to love and value us when we don't admire and cherish ourselves?

Accept that you've been insensitive to yourself in the past and moved on with a new awareness and a desire to love yourself. Self-betrayal healing means to embrace self-love. It's not a case of patience until you've figured out all your issues. Practicing self-love means thoroughly accepting yourself, unquestioningly, just as you are today. It means making choices of self-honor and telling oneself before you take any action, "Is this loving myself? Is this my highest meaning of love?"

The first person you wouldn't want to abandon, give up, or reject is you. Are your actions abandoning or rejecting you? Self-betrayal and self-abandonment are the reverse of self-acceptance. If you cheat, forsake, or deny yourself, you move away from love to fear. Love yourself is a remedy to many fears. Admiring yourself sets you free from toxic discourse in your mind. Repeatedly tell yourself the reality, "I am gorgeous, I am worthy, and I am likeable." And the time you consider this, you free yourself from the restraints of your brain that kept you trapped and restricted.

Show yourself the reality about your behavior, too. Take responsibility, stop being combative. Everyone is making bad choices. Accept your failures and be honest for telling yourself the reality. You're not your actions or your flaws. Yet, if you don't take care of them, you can never rise beyond your petty behavior. Take ownership and stop the accusation and the defense. It takes guts to speak the truth about it. Okay, be honest with yourselves. Without this, you cannot love or support yourself unquestioningly, so you remain trapped under the weight of deception, guilt, so justification. Free oneself with self-truth; that is the reality which defines your freedom.

Trauma
- Not A Fairytale

"Walking towards the future oh so bright
But little did she know that clouds of past trauma were awaiting for her in the starry skies in the name of rain"

Since the moment of birth, we've been told tons of stories about who we are. About who and how we're supposed to be. And then we begin to awaken slowly and surely. And then it's like a brain blast. The beginning of all the questions and all the stories we've got in our minds.

Trauma is that one unspoken voice, a deep well of memories which are suppressed or we can say memories which we are forgotten with time. Trauma is like a haunt or a caution board for the future. Trauma can indeed come from seeing someone be killed or seriously injured, either from learning about anything horrible that happened to a person we love. Trauma is that emotional damage which has a major impact on our lives. The trauma caused by another human in the form of an assault, death of a loved one.

A traumatic experience is an incident that causes physical, emotional, mental, spiritual or psychological harm. An individual who experiences a disturbing incident may feel disturbed, nervous, or scared as a consequence. In some cases, they may not learn how to react, or they may deny the impact that an incident has had. Little did we know that how the events happened in the past or maybe in childhood could hit us so hard that things get difficult with time!

Childhood. The very term paints pictures of innocence, happiness, positivity and wonder. Childhood is a time of safety-to be guarded and adored. Getting consistency in knowing that you are safeguarded by your family allows us to build stable and reliable relationships over time. It's really the ideal experience of childhood. However, the truth of many children's development and their effect on the rest of their lives are in marked contradiction to this idealistic assumption. Childhood Traumatic experiences can take a number of forms. As adults, we are often unable to handle these life events.

Imagine the size and reach of the child's eyes, trying to process the complexities of these experiences. And they try to understand their role in their occurrence. Kids do not process information by education, socialization, and life-experience as we do.

Childhood trauma chips away at a child's stability and sense of self, undermining self-worth and often staying with the child into adulthood. This trauma may also affect an individual as they experience feelings of shame and embarrassment, felt lonely and therefore unable to respond to anyone else, trouble controlling emotions, increased depression and anxiety, rage.

People react in multiple ways to traumatic events. Sometimes there are no obvious symptoms, yet individuals may have severe emotional responses. Shock and disbelief is a natural response shortly after the event. Shock and disbelief are often used to shield themselves against the emotional consequences of the event. You may feel numb or disconnected. You cannot notice the full force of the incident right away. Whenever the children's sense of self is damaged, it takes years of effort to rebuild the broken fragments and restore themselves to trust. Trauma, of course, doesn't just stop when someone becomes an adult. The human brain develops quickly between the ages of 0 and 6 years, and often the damage becomes ingrained into the subconscious of the child. Most times when we have hurt inner child, we are so used to feeling out of control that-without knowing-we build behavioral mechanisms to help us regain a sense of balance. An adult recovering from traumatic abuse is often unaware of how it affects their life – the reason is that recalling similar traumatic memories is hidden deep in the subconscious. Stories abound about people who experience painful flashbacks after a therapy session. Although a critical step in the healing process, it could be difficult to recall trauma events.

Trauma is one of the most crucial event which a person might face. It leaves deep emotional damage. Deeper the damage the more time it takes to heal. But we heal don't we? Just like a cut from a knife which heals with time. But it does take patience. Healing isn't an overnight process with an end goal it is an on-going process.

Emotions, perceptions, trauma — all living in our bodies and it's going to stay there unless we've processed it and got to the underlying cause of our pain.

Life will always throw obstacles at all of us which will have a massive impact and need careful consideration. There's still going to have something old that's going to be activated, that needs aggressive processing. Yeah, after 'waking up,' we can continue a healing journey. Yes, we will make some great steps. Sure, we can deactivate triggers and feel much less worried or anxious regarding it. Yes, of course, we can heal our pain.

Healing from trauma isn't easy. For recovering from childhood trauma, we need to complete the process that should have begun decades ago, when the incident occurred. Start with baby steps Like recall it, name it, accept it, share it and let it go.

Imagine a situation you've been upset about recently. Recognize something that triggered a moderate to powerful emotional reaction, even whether you won't look mentally numb. Take a look at what happened with as much depth while you can, and visualize oneself back in those times and places. Experience all of this again with the senses. When emotions begin to surface, start breathing the best exercise to calm yourself. Recognize any physical reactions you experience — tingly, stiffness, pain, etc. Each of these stimuli is a piece of knowledge that you need to grasp your past experience.

Now try to name it, it could be anxiety or rush of emotions in your mind. When the aspect of a mature approach to the healing of trauma, we have to simply acknowledge everything that we feel. Whether or not this is real to your conscious awareness during that moment, say, "I love myself for feeling (upset, sad, nervous, etc.)." Do this with any emotions you have, especially the rough ones. Embrace your faith, and love yourself for it. After you have embraced and loved each and every bit of yours with the emotions you feel let it go.

The process of healing emotional wounds can feel uncomfortable at first, but I promise it will be a very rewarding journey. The energy we currently spend on trauma will be released, and the space inside ourselves that trauma took up can instead be filled with new, more positive energy that can help us build a life that we will love.

"You are a warrior, you will fight and win this battle, stitch all those wounds of trauma and emotional damage. You will heal and come with a million dollar smile"

Trauma leaves us with invisible bruises and imprints.

ANXIETY
- MOSTLY OF unHAPPINESS

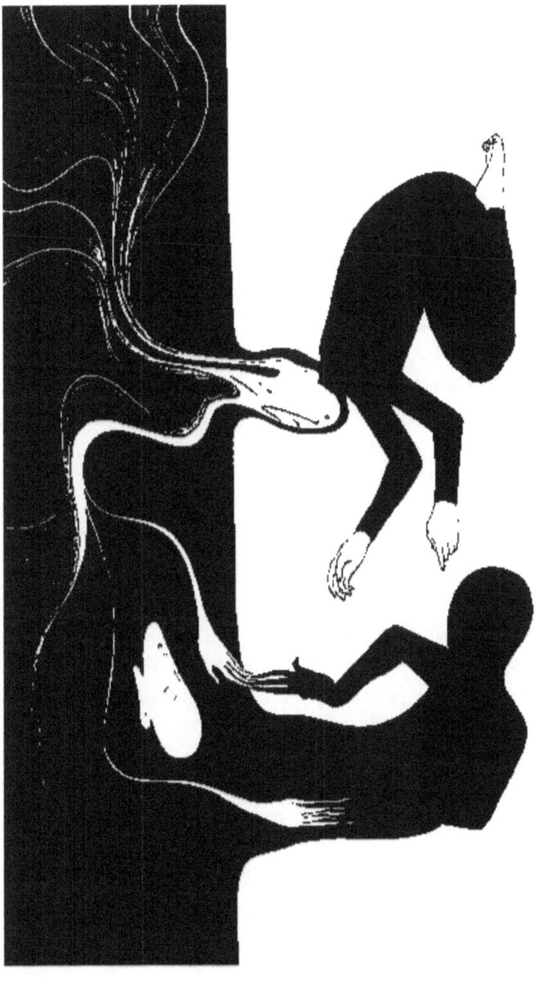

If someone ever confesses they have an anxiety disorder, do not even tell them they "just might need to relax." Because if it was that easy, I believe we'd have figured that out by now.

Just like how we are confused between depression and sadness we are confused between stress and anxiety. The disparities among stress and anxiety can be hard to spot from outside searching in. It could lead to nights of sleeplessness, fatigue, negative emotions, loss of concentration and irritability. Also symptoms – such as increased heart rate, tension in the body, and fatigue – can impact both people with depression and those dealing with an anxiety disorder.

In brief, stress is the reaction of your body to a stimulus, and is general an experience of a near term. Stress can have adverse effects. It is good when tension settles in and lets you pull off the deadlines that you thought was a hopeless case. It's bad when stress leads to insomnia, poor concentration and impaired ability to do the things you usually do.

Anxiety, in contrast, is a persistent mental health disorder that can be triggered by stress. Whenever the danger is resolved fear does not disappear into the distance. Anxiety hangs around for the foreseeable future, and can cause serious impairment in social, occupational, and other life stressors.

Let's live through a life of a person dealing and living with Anxiety.

Anxiety is that one demon which is not visible but still can be felt .Anxiety makes you feel like a blank slate. Some days your body is completely tense and your feet and hands feel like pins and needles. Feeling like that you have forgotten something essential and can't remember what it is, you get it out of bed. This anxiety can last the whole day, and can make me abnormally annoyed. It makes it very difficult to focus on the activities but often makes me as though my head is in the clouds.

You tend to be very rebellious on such days. Your heart flutters in your chest and the pain of familiar pins and needles spread over your body.

The firetruck alarms made me bolt out of my skin. The overstocked shelves in the library makes you feel like they were closing in on you in a blur of colors. Your heart races and your teeth grit and grind together. You have cold hands and feet often or your palms sweat.

On the way to a party, you would suddenly start shaking in the taxi or struggle to answer the phone but it seems terrifying. You can feel your mind losing and slipping; emotions keep continuously swirling and you keep experiencing visions of death in your eyes. You start experiencing suicidal thoughts. You realize this weight you constantly carry with a smile. It is exhausting. Your heart feels like an iron which keeps weighting and it causes you pain, so unbearable.

It is like you try to enjoy the ride. But instead, it feels like you`ve boarded the roller coaster where everyone else`s safety harness is secured but yours is broken and to which no one takes a note and then the ride takes off while everyone's hands are up and they are having enjoying, you`re just hoping your able to hold on until the end. Anxiety manipulates everything within you.

Anxiety amplifies your daily situations; you wake up anxious, so anxious that when you run towards the bathroom and it makes you feel horrible as well it makes you feel that bed is only the safest place for you. The worst feeling is that you can't breathe. Your heart starts pounding so fast you could feel it in your throat, it makes you feel you'll die in a moment and you feel like just running out of it ,but you still can't. Everything suddenly becomes loud and bold.

You feel like you are performing on stage and people are watching you every single second. You feel small and weak and overpowered. Your own life looks like a nightmare to you. There are nights when you are afraid, you sleep and feel worried that what if you get stuck in dreams and never wake up.

You cry under the shower, your tummy feels like a knot, you tremble inside. You only have to cope with yourself. You wake up from bad dreams every half an hour. You feel choking on your tears.

Living with anxiety isn't fun if it is equal to ruined relationships, social gatherings and good-byes to enjoyment. It is all about uncertainty because you don't know what will trigger you or when you'll have a panic attack.

Throughout the day you just wait for the day to end so you can hit the bed and feel safe and secure. Your existence becomes exhausting. Even the slightest change in your day eats you up and makes you feel super uncomfortable. Most of the memorable and joyful moments of life, your memories are tinged with a gripping, dark cloak of fear.

Furthermore, it can be really difficult to live with anxiety. It makes living your life almost impossible at times because the simple act of leaving your house may cast off an attack. It seems like the whole world intervenes to make you feel like total shit and you never know when it will happen. So in future If someone ever confesses they have an anxiety disorder, do not even tell them they "just might need to relax." Because if it was that easy, I believe we'd figured that out by now.

Anxiety is like a demon. Difficult to spot from outside. A demon how eats you from within. It's an invisible demon who makes you feel like a blank slate.

Living with Depression - Not an Easy Life

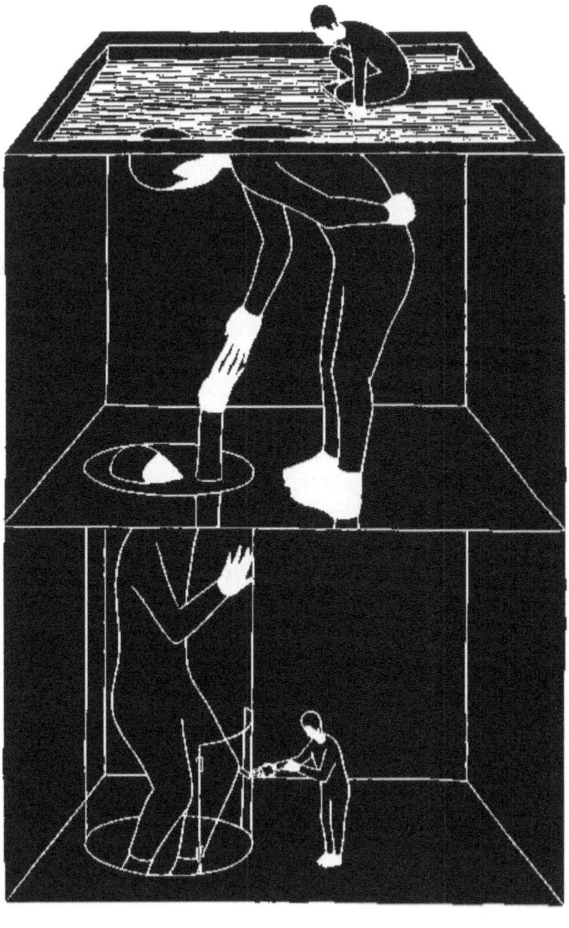

Bridging the gap here I go From insanity to sanity that's what people tell me to do because oh no depression is just overthinking you know.

Well, that's what we say ? Don't we ? or we say it's just that you're feeling sad. Sadness and depression are way too different. Sadness is something that isn't severe but depression is constant, persistent. Saying that depression is just about feeling sad, is just like saying 'the flu is only about sneezing' we know that flu isn't about sneezing with it comes fever and what not.

Sadness is a hallmark of depression. Another main distinction between grief and depression, however, is degree difference. Individuals suffering from depression experience a very serious level of sorrow. Depression also lasts longer than daily sadness. For an hour out of your day, depression is not feeling sad. It is not to be glorified. It is not perfect. Depression is at the brink of weeping, because you lost your water glass. It's not having the urge to clean up a mess, instead you're falling on the floor and sobbing uncontrollably. At times, it is a feeling where you're not brushing your hair makes you feel fine.

Depression is one excessive to another, maybe you are so high with happiness or so low that you doubt the color of the universe again. Some days are extremely decent, awesome and you almost feel like you're better. Just anything tiny will turn you into a wreck, a look from someone or a recollection. People will ask why you cry? What's wrong, then? And the only immediate reaction you can give is 'I don't know, but it isn't new.

There would be the days when you get out of your bed and yesterday's mascara will get you black underneath your eyes. That it is there, because the night before you didn't have the energy to clean off your makeup. Getting up and being ready for the daily routine gets difficult. You feel drained even if you have just woken up. Showers seem painful you're standing under the shower feeling numb and empty. The voices inside are screaming on the top of the voice wanting you to scream it and burst out. But stand still with no reaction on the face.

While you're working in your office cubicle and suddenly those tears start flowing which gets difficult to stop. Depression is a pain which is worse than any of the physical pain or scars. It feels like you are locked up in the dark room with no space for light and where you don't find any abscond from it and only feel that darkness has no end. It suffocates you from within.

It feels completely pointless to live, it feels like you're sinking in a tub of darkness with thorns pinching you on the back. It feels like suddenly the world around you just changed to something which you thought never existed, a feeling where the world suddenly just turned its back on you. When you look around yourself, all you could think is how are these people so joyful and happy? You question because the darkness within you shows no purpose of being happy, your perspective towards life changes and you start finding people crazy.

It feels like slitting up your wrists and ending it all for once. You can only see darkness and no joy in the moment or in the future. A feeling of being trapped in the maze and difficult to come out. Things get unbearable. It feels like living in hell where your inner voices become your own demons. You're too tired to move your head as it always feels heavy, you can feel your heart sinking. Your mind becoming a battleground, a constant fight with the pain.

For a moment you're happy and then you want to die. It takes too much space . It feels like you are drowning deep into the sea, you are choking, but you are not dying. And people are yelling at you to swim out of it like being a bird with clipped wings, while you watch everyone fly, it feels like you are colorblind and constantly being told how colorful the world is.

Depression is Dark, because the light has gone. Cold, because the warmth has left. Empty, because the water has drained, feels like you're watching your life from the passenger seat. Depression just feels like nothing. You're just feeling like you don't want to live but you're scared of dying. Much as you don't want out of bed because you're so depressed.

You're hungry but you're not able to wake up. You have to use the toilet but you don't want to get up.

You are just lying there. Feeling empty and sad. Just trying to finish it, feeling useless. And in every moment hazing yourself. And you believe you deserve pain because you're slicing. You want someone to ask for help but what is everybody going to think? Were you just being dramatic? It is tough.

Often you wonder if it's worthy trying to put on the same synthetic smile every day because you always feel worse yet you can't let anyone else know that so you sob in silence and want to die yet fear death. When you struggle to survive, and when you cherish death way more than life, that's exactly how depression feels like. This is what feels like living with depression means.

Depression isn't enjoyable, it isn't a game, and adding to your personality isn't a quirk, because you think it's cool. Depression is severe and ugly, and affects so many. Depression doesn't just go anywhere, you don't wake up unexpectedly and you decide not to feel helpless. It's all right crying out. It's good being poor. You are not just bulletproof, you are just a human. You will get hurt.

Feel the crap. Just work it out. Heal every tear. Mourn. Grieve. Shed tears. Cry out your heart, and destroy your mascara. Stop pretending. Unconceal yourself. When you're tired, collapse. Take a break. Get lost in the isolation you battled inside. You're doomed. ADMIT IT. Stop pretending for the first time that you're perfect. And let the curve be sadness on your face, instead of smiles. Let all of that out. Believe if you so desire. It's all right. Be miserable. You'll be healed with time. And then, take on with your life. Leave all of the suffering right from the tears you shed. Let's hold the memories but the good ones not the ones with pain. Smile: Smile. Smile the smile, without pretensions and heartbeats. Okay. Be fine. Be firm. Be fixable. Be glad. Live. Live. Start it on.

Do not judge the problems of other people, please listen to what they have to say. Their canyon may be a pile of rocks to you, but all are different and the feelings of all are valid. Please bear that in mind at all times.

Self-Harm
- The Beginning of the End

Self-harm is difficult to comprehend, as it goes against the natural human self-preservation instinct. This is maybe why certain people will respond to it in a harsh, judgmental way. They can't really imagine being in a mental state where they'd harm themselves, and they can't comprehend why anybody else would. This lack of awareness can lead to insensitivity and stigma against people who already struggle with severe emotional distress already.

Self-harm is usually a sign that a person has a hard time coping with their emotions. One big myth about self-harm is it's a suicide attempt. Self-harm is however a serious concern. And it's related almost always to some form of emotional distress. The act of intentionally hurting your own self, like cutting or burning yourself, is self-injury. It is not intended as an attempted suicide. Self-injury is also an unhealthy way of coping with emotional pain, intense frustration and anger.

Talking about Self-harm the first thing which comes to our mind is the cuts on the wrist. Am I right or am I right? The voices in your head are stronger than ever. Self-harm is done because that person feels he deserves it. At times it could be built-up guilt, frustration, pain, anger, emotions and what not.

Sadly, often emotional and mental pain is harder than physical pain as you may not always be likely to love the emotional or mental pain, and it is often easier to see the pain externally. You start feeling physical pain is far better than the emotional pain. Your head fills up with stress and anxiety which just gets uncontrollable. It keeps you pushing onwards the cliff and your visions get blurry.

It may feel like a release in the short term but in the long term it just drives you deeper and deeper into that dark place. You cut your wrist not to feel the pain but just to see yourself bleed, standing in front of the mirror, your liner all smudged and you see the blood dripping the voices in the background go inaudible and all you can hear at that point is the sound of the blood dripping.

You harm yourself not to die but have control over the pain. You cause self-harm to control your anger/feeling of hopelessness. The internal wounds start taking control of your mind. You start hurting yourself during those short bursts of really emotional times or even the hottest shower. You always want your outsides to hurt as much as my insides do. You start taking the mirrors away! You don't understand. You say you can't stand to see yourself. Everything in your life starts looking like trauma.

Self-harm becomes an easier way to explain it is to say that it's blinding mental pain with physical pain. For a while, you get out of your head and things seem real again. It feels like an addiction, you start to rely on pain for comfort. Self-harm is a vicious cycle that's really hard to stop. It becomes a release to you. Like you can finally BREATHE and your head becomes clear and it lifts the fog. You feel extremely down and numb, you get just desperate to feel alive. And as the blade slides down, you feel a surge of warmth that evaporates the numbness.

Anybody who harms self has different reasons & life experiences. It's not something that's easy to make sense of, but perhaps the last taboo is being a self-harming mother. It's covered up by the weight of shameful feelings, terror and secrecy; judgement inflames the stigma & drives this behavior further.

Self-harm may also be helpful coping release when people have no other way to cope with it but the issues that lead them to deal with it should be discussed rather than the act itself alone. Most often, the intention is to punish themselves, express their frustration or relieve intolerable pain and being unable to cope with it. Often it's a combination of all three, but that doesn't make them a terrible person or an unfit person.

We as individuals need to understand that no one on this fucking planet harms oneself for attention or to look cool. We aren't facing what they are facing. Scars always aren't the ones which are visible. Be it physical or mental scars- every scar has its own story. Your scars, speak every story. They show just how powerful you are.

They exemplify just how beautiful and worthy you are. Not to be ashamed of them but rather be proud of them. Don't hide them. If you suppose other people aren't going to like you because of your scars- STOP!!!

The right people will welcome you for who you are-they won't care about your past mistakes, weaknesses or wrong decisions. Get out of your own direction, and leave your doubts apart. Up until this point you have lived every precious minute of your life even when you believed you couldn't. You are a Warrior, a survivor. A warrior who stitched his own wounds, even with the teary eye.

We have to look far beyond wounds, drop the judgment and consider replacing it with compassion. Just remember not to focus on the self-harm, but instead on the person & what lies behind their misery. If you are struggling with this behavior, reaching out and discovering healthier ways of coping is important. Recovering can be a slow and painful process but, with support, it can be accomplished.

Sympathy & Empathy - A Confusion

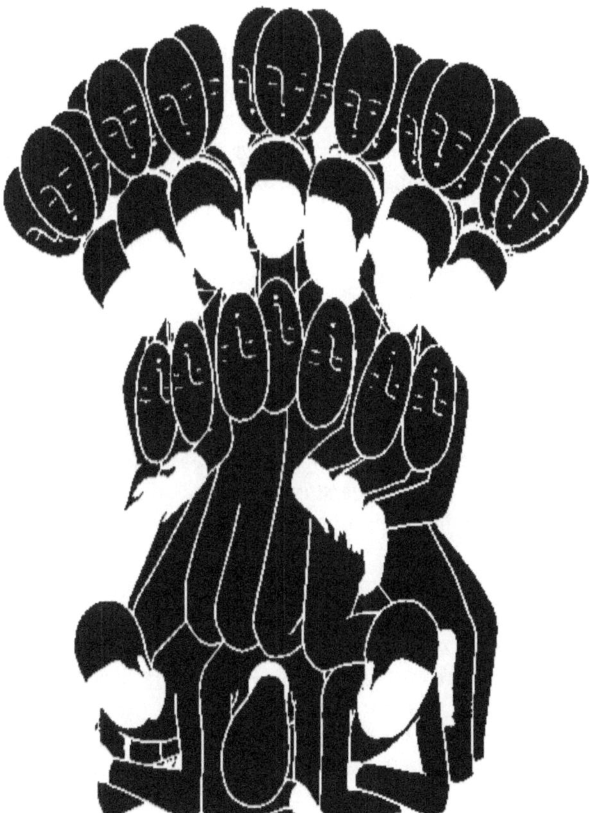

"Bruises all over my mind,
Damage which can't be seen and pain that I cannot hide,
you might empathize
but please don't sympathies
Come let's walk in each other's shoes
and feel everything that we go through"

Just as pleasure, sorrow and despair are different for each individual and the meaning in that, they are felt and there's empathy. There are therefore many elements of empathy that literally come from the German word "Einfühlung" which means "feeling in." As just as there are many reasons to feel; there are also several ways to perceive and express compassion.

Empathy and sympathy are two words that you hear bound around a lot, but then what do they necessarily imply, and how are they distinct from one another? It's something that perplexes a large number of people which is often used synonymously. The reason for this is that they all deal with the individuals personal ability to understand the feelings and emotions of others. Empathy is way more than I hear You, it is a feeling where you put yourself into someone's shoes and walk a mile and hopefully that's when we understand what the other person feels like or understanding the situations that person is dealing with.

It's real that if we step into yet another person's situation or visualize what that person is feeling or experiencing. Empathy extends far above emotion, that might be considered to be 'feelings' toward others. Empathy is what facilitates pro - social behaviors or, in other words, helps actions that tend to come from the inside and also isn't pressured. This makes us a more empathetic society that is willing to recognize each other's feelings and take action. Empathy, on the one hand, is 'feeling for' the individual by the use of imagination.

Empathy stands in stark contrast to sympathy, which is the willingness to truly understand the perspective or emotion of an individual, but it is without the emotional overlay that comes with it. We should also make sure that it is distinguished from love, while both are used in the same way.

Empathy and sympathy are embedded in the concern for the well-being of others. Perhaps the best way to understand empathy is to put yourself in the shoes of another person, a reference to the old idiom, 'walk a mile in your shoes before you judge a man.' Empathy develops as you, yourself, seek and grasp and sense the feelings of another person as if they were your own.

I feel your pain" is more than a metaphor. It's literal

To make the shoe metaphor concrete, imagine if you will see someone drop anything huge on their foot—you flinch as you understand what that looks like, and the bits of your brain that feel pain. You don't experience the same degree of discomfort, of course — you didn't drop something on your feet after all — but you probably have an unpleasant physical response like a shiver, a facial scowl, or an audible scream. That's an emotionally empathic response.

Sympathy, on the other hand, is an emotion of grief for someone else's misery. You feel so terrible for others regardless of their situation or events. Sympathy is often full of clichés and closely linked to empathy. The word has negative connotations for many. The distinction between the two terms may seem slight, but it is equivalent to two vastly distinct forms of behavior and emotion. Sympathy often does or says what is anticipated, which is why the infinite supply of sympathy cards. Whereas, on the other side, empathy follows the golden rule, 'Treat others as you would like to be treated.'

Well, It comes as no surprise that being empathetic is a very valuable skill. We might have discussed our personal issues with our mates. At times we get answers that leave us feeling worse and makes us deeply regret discussing our issue.

Whereas, sometimes when we make causal statements some people would grab, which later turned into heart-felt discussions. Unless you are empathetic towards others, you can't help them feel better for themselves. You let them know that they're not there alone in their difficulties. You also strengthen your connection with the person, and then when you seek to convey emotions to another, you allow the thoughts and emotions to circulate between the two of you.

When it comes to empathy, show concern, acknowledge the feeling of that person, be a pillar to that person, be their strength last but not the least support them emotionally. Encourage them. Let them know that no matter what happens, you have their back in every situation, any obstacle. Sometimes, what people are looking for is not answers or solutions to their problems. Sometimes, all people are looking for is empathy ,love and support. That in this big world of unknown, loaded with anxiety and doubt, there is someone here just to help them, without discrimination or prejudice.

Black Rainbow
- Another phase of Life.

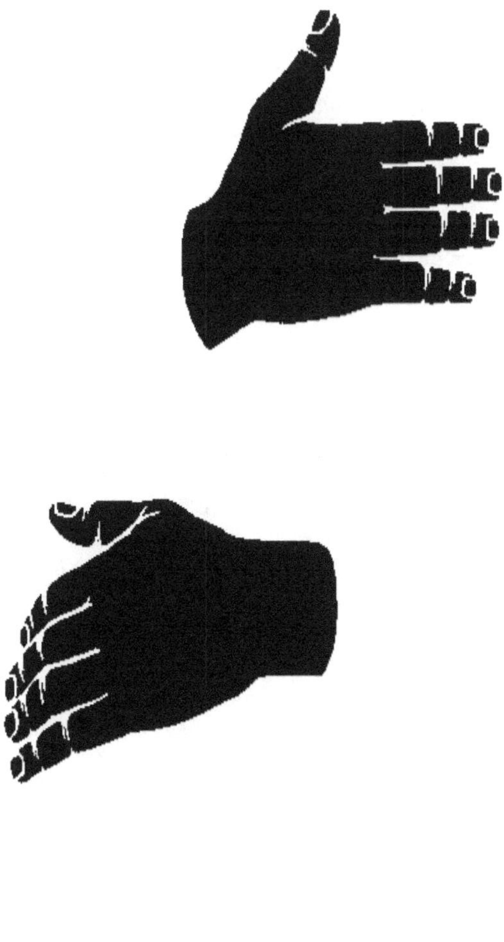

We all have different chapters in our lives. Some turn out to be the best whereas some turn out to be the worst. But, from each chapter and each mistake we learn and grow from it. Why hate life? For our own mistake. Every time we fell we stood up. Because dark clouds don't last forever. They last only if we let them stay.

Someone told me Like a rainbow after a rain, there's always a good thing after the pain. So yes this chapter too had pain but it taught me a lesson. Life is pretty long, and we have a lot to do to achieve goals and much more. It might take some time to move on, maybe some days or some months, but we move on eventually. Yes, we are young, and we make mistakes but that doesn't mean that we always can. I found magic and love within myself and it's difficult to love someone else when you can't love your own self. With every passing day, I'll fall in love with myself, pick those broken pieces and rise like a Phoenix bird.

It happened for a reason and it's okay not be okay at times but definitely I'll be okay. There also might be days when I'll cry, but it's okay to cry out rather than bottling up things. After all we all deserve happiness. Why hate someone when love can do it's magic. Embrace your life the way it comes. Do what makes you happy, live the moment, fall in love, party, do whatever makes you happy even if it's wrong but makes you happy do it but be ready to face the circumstances later. Go pet some dogs, gift yourself do whatever it takes to make yourself fall in love with your own soul. And if it gives you lemon, throw them back or just have it with a shot of tequila.

Hope
- A Voice Within

Hope should unlock the gates, when disappointment blows. 'Hope' as an effective survival tool. There is life until hope is alive. It doesn't feel like this when you are located in the midst of a tough situation. It feels like you're pushing the wind from your sail and all you want is to give up. No situation can kill you, but there is one thing that will stop you: hopelessness.

The overwhelming sense that there's no way out is despair. It sees no potential to turn the desired outcome into reality. Hopelessness shades your perspective so as to see only the gaping gaps, absurdities and what not. Since your brain is able to see if it already knows to be true, it feeds itself on helplessness. The less optimistic you feel, the less hopeless you feel, the less faith-filled authority you use to affect your scenario. As issues grow when faith no longer influences them, it seems to confirm the hopelessness. It is a fall to the downside. It's hard to keep going, without hope.

Without the belief that winning is possible your power will be depleted long before the battle begins. If there is no good on the horizon, your moves already are exhausted even before the journey begins. Hope sees what is achievable and all that's left without it is an overwhelming sense of implausibility. Hope is just what makes you feel that it's worth it. Some efforts lacking in it is believed to be in doubt, and it feels too much to handle. Be it any situation the beauty of the dark times is that we all have a ray of hope, a voice within which tells you not to give up.

Be it anyone or any situation. Since we are talking about mental health whenever the darker side of your mind pushes you to give up on yourself or the situations always believe yourself that the situations will get better and it's just a difficult and a rough patch which you're going through we know there are days when you can only see darkness ahead of you but don't let the light within become dim and make you blind on your path because at the end of the road there is a bright light waiting for you to win the race with all the ups and downs.

Don't give up. Believe in the ball of hope, look at how far you have come letting the pain go off, all the struggles, the trauma. Things will get better, brighter and much more beautiful. Hope is what shows you it's worth it. Hope is unique for every individual. Perhaps some of you are reading this right now hoping that you'll get the job you've applied for or that we'll get our last bit of sunshine before it's officially winter. You may also be finding it hard with your mental wellbeing and keep the very same / related hopes for yourself. Hope can come from our inner desire to heal health and live again. It can also come from the reassurance of people who actually care about us. The more involved we are in understanding our situation, taking full responsibility for our own wellbeing and seeking help, the more chances we have to make progress that offer us a greater justification for doing so.

I will rise in flames,
Those which no one can tame,
I will leap from my own fire,
My grace and elegance shall everyone admire

Acceptance
- A Step Towards Healing

Acceptance a struggle for humankind. A struggle yet a step towards healing "A baby step". Acceptance is essential, it unlocks the skepticism, fear, and cynicism of a situation or obstacle that we may face by opening the door for us to face it head on. In other words, acceptance is about facing the reality.

So often we feel trapped in the mire of uncertainty, unable to control results, acceptance is a habit that can profoundly impact our ability to make positive change. Many people consider the word 'acceptance' to mean reluctance by connecting it to complacency.

Actual acceptance is quite the opposite, it is a matter of finding the clarity to recognize and face our complexities and uncertainties, which is more of a sign of courage. life is unpredictable and that transition is bound to happen, resistance to it seems ineffective. Acceptance, moreover, is the power that we give ourselves to move peacefully through challenges. Acceptance means that you have to accept who you are not who you think you should be. It also means that you have to acknowledge your positive qualities and your bad ones. And yes, we do have both positive and bad qualities.

Somehow this topic is very dear to my heart, and somewhere or someplace, all of us reading it will be connected to it. Anything that is wisdom and it's something that we all struggle with, "Importance of Acceptance"

Here you would relate — when terrible things happen, a lot of people will say, "I just can't even believe it," or I just honestly can't believe it like that, or even this can't happen to me. We're investing so much hope and energy in scenarios that we tend to believe and get carried away by what we think, idealize or wait and create a bubble of self-delusion that's just about to pop. That's when we ought to see things as they are. "I have been living in the bubble of delusion to be honest"

Let's take an example: Separation from a loved one puts you in a situation where you keep thinking why me ? Why did it end? Where did I go wrong? And many more questions keep popping up. How many more downhill's do I have to cross?

Acceptance is not only about accepting yourself but also about accepting the situations and relationships. None of us are perfect. Actually perfection is a Myth. When we accept ourselves and the situations with its positives and negatives that's when we can say it's perfect.

But you know what? Every negative things or such situations have something positive in it. But do we ever sit down and think about the positives of the situation? It helps you realize your strengths even better. Most of the situations we experience in our day-to-day life are a combination of good, bad, and weird. Always realize that something good comes out of acceptance. Always remind yourself – but in a different way, we need the experience to learn the good lessons we've learned from life. The more you embrace it, the more you know about yourself. Over the years, we learnt that we can conquer any journey as long as we are willing to take a step at a time. We don't have to fix everything at once, just concentrate on the never-ending To-Do list in your mind.

But we end up doing the complete opposite and we just keep thinking about it. The more we think about it, more the situation gets worse. It undoubtedly takes time, acceptance is a journey which needs to be undertaken for sake of our own happiness and peace of mind. When we talk about acceptance, it could be a concern of the slightest thing to something that might make a change in the world, and then when we talk about a minor thing, it could be a matter of our daily struggle to accept ourselves, our bodies, our family and friends, and, most importantly, the life we live. When we speak about embracing ourselves, it may be something as simple as the shape of your nose, weight, color or even situation.

Acceptance begins with every one of us. If we can't master to accept ourselves first, we're going to spend our lives being bitter to the rest of the world, instead of trying to do what we can to make it a better place.

It's time for us to accept our differences, use them to tie us together rather than tearing us apart. Everyone needs to embrace themselves for who we really are, because only then the world will see you as nothing less, and most importantly, it shouldn't matter what the world sees, the world can see you like a teacher, a kid, or a drama queen, and never something that you really stand for, so avoid making an acceptable picture of yourself in world, it will just look at you the way it wants.

So, where else are we going from here? Let us just open our eyes, our ears, and our hearts, because acceptance is the starting point. Lastly, "Jab hum apne aap ko achhi tarah samajh lete hai, to dusre kya samajhte hai, it doesn't matter. Not at all!"

HEALING
- A GOODBYE TO OLD WOUNDS.

The journey of healing isn't as easy as it sounds. Trying to recover from mental illness involves not only improving but fulfilling a complete and rewarding life. Many people say their path towards recovery wasn't a simple, steady path. Instead there are highs and lows, new findings and setbacks. With time, it's important to look back and see how far we have actually come, given the halting progress and disappointments.

Coupled with such losses, the pain of mental illness can be unbearable. At some moment, however, we find the willingness to stop sustaining and begin to reincarnate, bit by bit. That's when recovery begins. Care should be based on finding the correct diagnosis and relieving the most serious symptoms early in the recovery phase. At this initial stage, it is important to understand that having help from people that understand what you are going through is crucial.

Family, friends, the communities of faith, self-help organizations and community groups may all be of support. You may consider yourself in another recovery phase with the passing of time. Your condition is getting more stable. There is so much that can contribute to this improvement: appropriate treatment, accurate medication, supportive talk therapy, and your own basis of growth of your condition and how to enjoy living with it. Once it was assumed that this health level was as far as it could go for people with mental illness.

The objective of treatment was to maintain stability. But, we understand today that a more great deal is possible. You should anticipate your dreams, interests and skill to return to an active life. Recovery of any illness, trauma or anything that occurs in your life is full of road bumps. It's not going to be a tough path, if it was then you as a person might not be able to grow, not only psychically, but emotionally and mentally. If you can't grow by what you've seen, you will not be able to live to the fullest.

The events we're going through, whether in our work or personal life, allow us to grow and emerge bigger. In other words, we wouldn't even be able to develop as individuals without them.

Healing is never easy, you may witness numerous ups and downs or maybe even withdrawal symptoms but it doesn't mean you should quit. It really doesn't mean that you may have given up on life, that failure comes to everybody but in various ways.

I am a strong believer that in order to get ahead you have to fail. It is one of life's series building blocks and it's something we need to remember every day. Healing is a recovery process since you pull yourself through all the hardships that have mentally, physically and emotionally impacted you. They push you to the limit and it is here that your healing begins.

When dealing with recovery, you need to realize that healing is a process of recovery, and that it will take time. It takes several weeks, months , and years until you begin to understand this. For self-care, that's also important to remember, initiating the effort for a happy and healthy life and seeking recovery is essential. Many people have life experiences that test and drag them to the threshold through painful and difficult times but one thing in common is that they derive from these encounters. Recovery is the best way to cure your scars completely whether they would be physical, emotional or mental. Choose the path and you take the correct steps to live a better and happier life, not only for yourself but also for those surrounding you. You'll find so much love , hope, and support in choosing the path to recovery. As many people do, it is not a show of failure but a sign of strength because facing all the experiences again and accepting them and letting them go isn't easy.

I so wanna scream badly,
And cry out loudly,
Let this pain sink in my chest,
And I feel no regret,
It's killing me now,
And I'm healing that way somehow

Mental Health
- A Stigma to the Society

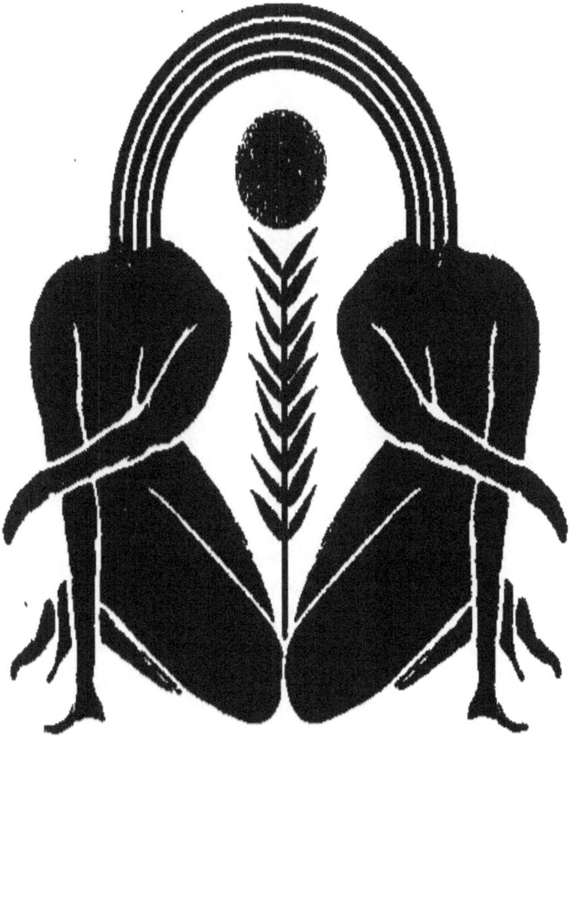

Let's admit it; people in today's world still have irrational and unfounded views about mental illness. Well, everyone knows that Mental Health still remains to be a stigma in our society just like having periods and LGBTQ isn't it. Yes, we do talk about it but what if someone from your friend circle or family faces a mental health issue will you accept it? Or say " Arre tum zyada soch rahe ho kuch din mein thik ho jayega? To us it might just be overthinking but to the person who is facing it is watching their whole life crashing and feeling and seeing themselves trembling from a cliff.

The people in our society often label them as psycho, maniac, lunatic and words which are really harsh. We aren't helping them in any way by saying all of it. Instead we are pushing them towards the cliff and forcing them to jump. All we are doing is just increasing the stigma around us. It is not to be shameful about having difficulties with mental health. It is just like another issue which any other part of your body may face. WHY DO WE CREATE SO MUCH OF NEGATIVITY ABOUT IT??

We make them build walls around themselves. Why do we make them feel embarrassed or shameful and look at them like they have done some crime. We make them lose out on the social support that they need. Why does talking about mental health makes us uncomfortable? Little did we know there are a huge number of people facing mental health issues, surprising isn't it? A person can still face mental illness without being sad; depression isn't the only mental health issue it is more than that. Not only that but it's not only the females who face mental health issues, males also go through such issues.

When a teenager feels low, it always doesn't mean it just because the puberty has hit him. Everyone in the world can face this issue not only the normal people; it could be a singer, actor or any celebrity as well. A person with mental illness is not aggressive well here. We should thank Bollywood for creating such an image of people with illness. It's high time now that we should start talking about it openly rather than running away from it.

People who face all these issues related to mental health avoid talking about it. Do we know why? Because they feel they themselves are inviting troubles. Well, in a way they are correct because we have spoken shit out of mouth right?

"Yaar tum toh defective piece ho" that's what we say or aisa kuch nahi hota"

Our most favorite statements and so much of judgements. Stigma and stereotypes make them feel worse. We need more of these stigma busters. Stigma is a word no one understands well enough. It's like racism. It's deeper than the beliefs people are conscious of. Discrimination is not only about race , gender or religious belief: it involves discrimination against people with mental health problems.

People prefer not to have a mental illness just like they choose not to be in a certain race. Ignorance about mental illness causes isolation and prevents sufferers from living life to the full. One in four people will have mental health problems at some point in their life, but many more have a problem with that. When people cannot distinguish the difference between mental illness and learning disabilities, it's disheartening.

The more stigmas, the less people will seek care". That is not accurate. Stigma is unquestionably still a significant issue. And we should avoid discriminating between mental disorders and other brain diseases. Yet to say the stigma is exactly the same-sorry to use this word anyway-mad.

Individuals actually need to realize exactly how much of a stigma a problem really is, and make a concerted attempt to do something about it. Thinking and living our lives knowing that the detrimental things we bring out in the world have a negative effect on people dealing with a mental health condition is not our duty but to target anyone and say that it is not our problem. Let's take a look at several things that hardly make any effort to make life less difficult for an individual.

Especially when the life of that person is already more challenging than should be. Rather than adding to their issues and making their lives harder, we must try and do our part to ease the difficulties people face. Let's make a difference. Be it in general, at the workplace, friends or family.

Recognize things for what they're really, rather than seeing them based on nothing more on your own opinion. Do not neglect the things you are saying and doing in regard to how they affect the lives of yet another person. Stop letting the media to manipulate your personal view, particularly by using biased one-sided views. Ought not to turn a patient's mental illness into a joke and the serious problems that go with it. Don't leave them feeling like they're a crappy person to sometimes deal with these situations ahead of your friendship. Don't beat them down for wanting help. Help them rather than treating them as if they are a burden, or simply want attention.

Please stop holding that against employees once they have psychiatrist visits, particularly if those appointments are for a continuing condition. Be compassionate, rather than making them feel less like an employee. When coping with a mental or physical disorder , a person should not have to feel bad or guilty; both are true health issues.

Respect your employees and colleagues if someone in the workplace expresses that they have been denigrated because of a work colleague. Treat it no differently than someone who discriminates against a person based on their gender or color. When anyone wants items that have been explained more than once or explained in another way, don't try to abandon them or make them feel dumb. Explain it so they understand, rather than threatening them.

Help your child learn its condition. Think at what you're doing to make their lives simpler and also what you're doing to make their lives tougher. Don't make them feel like they're a burden. Do things to help build up your child so others won't be able to break it down. Respect the limits. Don't make them feel bad or guilty for needing medication.

Mental health stigma is not a deficiency of character; mental disorder is a legitimate medical condition. Discrimination is difference based on race, religion, and ethnicity, and yes, mental illness. For some reason our society shows more hopelessness to mental health issues than empathy, which is something we're ashamed of, especially when the life of a person is perceived with so little value. We should be ashamed that we cannot see beyond our own uneducated opinions.

Burnt by my flashes,
Scorching myself,
My existence dwarfed like an elf,
All that is left of me are the ashes

WHY IS IT DIFFICULT TO OPEN UP ABOUT MENTAL HEALTH ILLNESS?

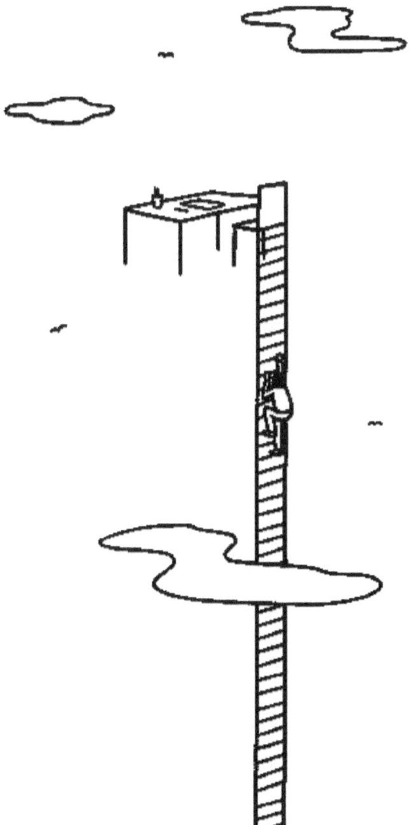

Mental illness is also Genuine. As someone living with a mental illness and as a supporter, ignorance has to stop. It's not safe in any way or it helps the society. It's not a process or something like that and there are millions of people suffering a mental illness but many fail to seek treatment because of misinformation which also makes things difficult for them. It also becomes difficult to express their feelings to us. Some of the major reasons are judgement, fear of being misunderstood, guilt and shame not being accepted.

Fear of being judged-To tell others about how we feel - particularly when we seem like the endless worry over every little thing is crazy - makes me very worried over how we will look to others. It is a very difficult task to explain to people the feelings that are going up there. Like we say it out loud, we can tell that we sound utterly irrational and naive, but what people do we think about when these words fumble from our lips?

Being misunderstood- fear of speaking up to others about the feelings and feeling utterly misunderstood. It scares us, really. It can also be very confining and unpleasant to deal with such things when you have a mental illness. If we start opening and the person doesn't get it or neglect what one is trying to say, it's like you got rejected for how you feel and that you are clearly stupid. If you reach that response, it makes you feel even more lonely and alone when it comes to dealing with this awful illness.

Guilt-If you are obsessively concerned over something that really isn't 'the end of the world' in the big scheme of things, there can be a sense of guilt and even embarrassment. This can be (and was) amplified when you opened up to these people and were told, "Everything could have been worse, think of those people in the world who are much worse than you" or the question was responded: How have you found to be really anxious about this though? ". When you experience anything like that, this can make it so much challenging to be honest about your real feelings, as it is accompanied by the thought that you really don't deserve to feel that way, that you'll just snap it out.

And it is not that fast, really. Even though for all of the reasons described you can find it difficult to open up to your loved ones about your illness, when you finally open up to let people know what's going on, it does make a huge difference. It feels like you could lift off your heavy thoughts and recognize though that your thoughts tell you that you are alone but you are not.

Fall in love with yourself with all your flaws. Because you're perfect with all your imperfections

#LETS_TALK!
TO THE NEW BEGINNINGS

There's nothing wrong with making a new beginning in life and that's what we should do at some point in our life. We can begin to make new improvements which will lead us on a new path through life. It's overwhelming, and at the same time one must be excited for such improvements. Start making the effort to a more happy, fun, self-loving and optimistic outlook. With every new step of our life, we must begin to make a more conscious effort for a mentally, physically and emotionally happy, more peaceful and more positive improvement. They have to make changes at some point in an individual's health but sometimes that needs to begin with a clean slate. But you might wonder how somebody can get off to a new beginning? What are some quick but necessary changes that an individual can make to start a fresh to a better life?

Accept change – The only thing which is constant is changes. Changes are important and sometimes starting over means, you let go of the person you were once.

Write about your past-It doesn't have to be large or small. It could be something that recently occurred or happened a long time ago so you need to get that out of there. We usually don't understand the power of journaling until we actually do. It helps you to let go of the emotions which hurt you and also helps you to understand your emotions in a better way.

Speak to somebody – tell them what you feel about your current situation in life. Talking help always works. Because we all need to be heard somewhere in our lives. (where there is no judgement)

Admit failure – For everyone including me, it's very tough sometimes but this is something that has to occur. Yeah, this does sting. Yes, it won't be that easy and therefore sometimes you're going to accept what's happened and is happening in your life with all of it. We need to accept failure and we need to move on.

Make peace with your past – Accept all your previous defeats and wins, past mistakes, failures, as well as other situations in life which have occurred. Let those in the past stay there, and drop it there.

All these are few other things one can look at trying to make a new and clean start. You don't have to do anything like that if you like, you can. Beginning fresh and clean is great. There is literally nothing wrong with that, in fact I believe it shows growth and determination towards a much healthier, happier and more fulfilling life. Leave the world behind you, and begin with a fresh outlook. It is also an essential gesture of self-care which is essential for an individual's mental, emotional, and physiological condition at any stage in our lives.

PAST- BIDDING GOODBYE

For many people like me, the past can be very traumatic. It may cause severe reminders of previous events that have taken place in the life of a individual which may cause them to revive old experiences. Although, the past can be very painful, you can learn from it too. Throughout our life we all make mistakes (including myself) ,mistakes where we actually didn't mean to hurt someone, some decisions and many more yes it does cause us some pain.

Past is like a difficult chapter especially for people who overthink and get anxious. The old chapters become like wounds and it gets difficult to talk about it. It may lead us to feel responsible, rethink the event or situation, and question if things could have been done differently. Although the past can sting, it can cure too. The past is a very tough thing but we grow from our mistakes. As humans, we will grow and mature emotionally, physically and psychologically.

We are always afraid to make mistakes when we grow up but the older we get, we begin to realize that learning from mistakes is all apart from life. Making mistakes is common, and because it is actually impossible, we cannot accomplish a life of perfection. Making mistakes is perfectly alright, we all do. It is an essential part of life. But, what some people are struggling with, Me as well, is moving on after making those blunders and embracing the past and having to leave the past behind.

Allowing letting go of all the past is not something that has been implemented quickly, but it takes baby steps. It's not easily done but could be accomplished with time, patience and acceptance. There will always be snapshots of the past. It's not as if they can be lost and I truly believe we should look back in time to see how much we have grown. The past is painful but it could also help with our lives to heal and move ahead. The past is a number of things but all of us have been shaped by past events in life which have psychologically, physically and emotionally altered us.

Don't let the past push you down the hill. Do not allow your past experiences to stop you from living in the present and looking towards the future.

YOUR JOKES- SOMEONE'S BATTLES

Pure and simple ignorance is the lack of understanding or information on a particular issue. What kind of issue am I talking about? Mental Illnesses and the associated stigma. They add to the stigma by talking about OCD, Anxiety, Depression, Bipolar, & other mental disorders. They are rude, improper, hurtful and insulting. It isn't about being too sensitive, it's mocking people who have undergone the trauma that people find entertaining. This is not a funny part, or a game. It is not about becoming too emotional for us not to be able to handle a joke. These are issues which no one should pun about. Just like anything else that is visually seen, these were all real issues. That's why there's stigma and awareness within the mental health system needs to be there. Those who suffer with a mental disorder shouldn't be taken as a joke by their struggles, but it's the real tragedy. It's not humorous to make others into a joke or style trend, and appears to lack decency on several levels. If people just took the time to understand mental illness and how a person's life can be severely impacted by puns.

The challenges are not humorous, demeaning and insensitive and lead many people to believe that we in the mental health system simply want attention if that is not the reality. Ignorance is ignorance, those who lack the knowledge and acceptance on this subject simply have to move back and look at themselves in the realization that not all wounds are evident. It is just as simple as this. Our disease is not intended for laughs. We are true and we don't describe our struggles. The comments add to the prejudice and that just isn't acceptable.

THE BRIGHT & DARK SIDE WITHIN

We have both darkness and brightness in us. It's just how we 're moving on something which describes us really. There are circumstances where emotionally, physically, and intellectually we are sorely tested and undoubtedly our reaction is the result of our thought pattern and behavior. Our choices sometimes have implications that we may not always expect but we learning from such consequences of actions can help us grow. Everything depends on the circumstances but this all relies about how we respond. For instance, if you find out someone you trust has gossiped about you, what will you do? Do you think about the situation first, or do you react first? This all revolves on how the situation is perceived. Which one is it you should do? Would you interrogate your friend and ask why he/she said things about you or are you going to fight back in another way? The gloom that fills us with feelings of anger, denial, envy often dampens our minds since we first think about the scenario and then find out how to react. What we respond to in the situation says it all. Often we will act before we think and both ways of thinking have different outcomes. Whether you respond first, you may end up dealing with repercussions you don't want, or if you think about the problem that is being posed to you, then you may have a better way of coping with the problem.

We all have a light and dark nature in us and we react differently to situations but I firmly believe that these situations will help a person to grow. Often, how you react to situations tells your maturity and the willingness to rise beyond. All of us are human, and that we are prone to feel conflicting feelings, and our thought process mechanisms are different, and are what makes us different. Undoubtedly, thinking already when you act can help you see a new aspect to issues, and also help to make your thinking process easier to understand. This is all about how you perceive the circumstance and how you want to use the light or darkness within you.

There are days when you look in the mirror where you can see both the sides the darker and the brighter one. Simple yet complex. On somedays, you look at the darker side where things seem too complex and when you only see your flaws you start believing it. But look at yourself finely look within look how far you have come winning all the battles, winning against all the society stereotypes.

Your struggles, battles but don't let them define YOU. There are good and bad days but you're better, braver, and stronger than all demons. One of the most important things you need to understand is to know that you are enough, you matter, you are doing everything and your best you can do. Self-care is the most important thing from all aspects of life. You can't serve an empty vessel. You need to refill your cup and go at your own pace. So heal. Look within you are an amazing person. The million dollar smile and the eyes which shine along lights up the world of someone who loves you. There are hard times in life and there are times when standing up gets difficult but that's when you have to look within. Somewhere within you'll find a Phoenix Bird who turns into ashes but still comes up as whole and when it comes out as whole is rises and shines much more wiser. Let the Phoenix inside you get stronger and wiser. Because you know what. YOU MATTER. YOUR EXISTENCE MATTER.

And Love Yourself For Who You Are.

I have felt for the longest time that loving someone is beyond any emotion that you may have for them. It turns out it is not. Often, "when you look ahead, you'll find people who love you but really don't like you and it's the world's loneliest feeling."-Bojack Horseman. So ,be rebelling in a world that benefits from your self-doubt. Be good on the hatred. Be gentle before getting rude. Place up open to cruel. Today, I write this for you as well as myself. I want you to believe more in yourselves. If you can, I want you to help out others. I want you to pick yourself up when you have to. I want you to do all you can, and make your dreams come true. I want you to have yourself loved. I want you to smile, until your jaw hurts.

If you found this book helpful to understand the stigma of mental health and related mental health disorders please leave a review on Amazon. I read every review and they help new readers discover my book.

Chandni Akhenia

a 23 year old chasing her dreams like every other girl. A BMM Advertising Graduate currently pursuing MA in Psychology and working as Digital Marketer and a Trainer. An introvert and a Bollywood buff, obsessed sunsets and pretty skies and DOGS. Memes and Dog pictures make me the happiest oh and food obviously.

Three years back I started with writing blogs just as college assignments. Isn't it like a turn of events that just from writing blogs I ended up writing a book which has always been a dream. Finally turning into reality. To me writing always came effortlessly. Writing, reading, sketching has always been my favorite thing to do.

THE MYTHICAL BIRD

"REBIRTH OF A PIOUS DAUGHTER"

The name of the book itself talks about the rebirth. The rise after the fall just like how Phoenix Bird burns itself into ashes and then rises much brighter, stronger and wiser. Just like how the Phoenix Bird is called the Mythological bird which no one has seen yet we talk about it. That's exactly the point there is is a lot of talking about the mental health yet less acceptance about it. Yes, we do talk about it on social media but what when you find your close one in the situation? We often talk only about the brighter side of life and not on the darker side. This book puts a light on the darker side of life. Things we don't often talk about.

The Mythical Bird is a phase a journey of Healing. A Journey of Ups and Downs. A Journey about how things begin related to Mental Health. How it all starts with a constant feeling of emptiness which turns into overthinking and how that overthinking turns into controlling and suppressing all our emotions and how the cycle goes on. How sympathy doesn't work always at times rather than sympathizing we should once place ourselves into shoes of someone who faces all of it. Look at life the way they look at life. Just for once lets go inside each other's minds feel and understand their battles and look at things with each other's eyes.

www.ingramcontent.com/pod-product-compliance
Lightning Source LLC
Chambersburg PA
CBHW050021170726
48282CB00025B/487
9788194673965